CONTENTS

WITHDRAWN

BECAUSE OF LOVE FRANKO B'S STORY

We all are survivors in one way or another.
Surviving is a must and not some kind of sport.
This is what we do because there is no other option.
There are no heroics or bravado here, there are no
medals to receive or to dish out for being 'here'.
There are no winners or losers, just other lives.

Franko B

INTRODUCTION
LOIS KEIDAN

Franko B is an extraordinary artist who has been making drawings, installations, sculptures and performances for over 30 years.

I have had the pleasure of working closely with Franko since I was at the Institute of Contemporary Arts in London in the 1990s, and he has been involved with, and indeed inspired, many aspects of the Live Art Development Agency's work since we set the organisation up in 1999. Franko has performed at some of our major events, spoken at many of our gatherings, and mentored numerous younger artists we have supported over the years. We have Franko's books on the shelves of our Study Room research library, sell his books and editions through our online shop, and hang his art on our walls. His presence and influence can be felt everywhere in our work.

Much of Franko's artistic practice, and particularly his performance work, could be seen as autobiographical, drawing on his lived experiences and expressing his personal politics in order to, as he has so often said, 'make the unbearable, bearable', and confront the human condition in its most vulnerable and carnal state.

The title *Because of Love*, however, refers to an explicitly autobiographical body of works. The first version of *Because of Love* was a performance Franko created in 2012. It was his first stage-based work, in which he performed scenes from his life, particularly his troubled childhood, and used the texts from an earlier attempt to narrate his life story as a vocal score sung by Mitch Miller. This was followed in 2016 by the film *Because of Love*, a collaboration with filmmaker Nathaniel Walters made over a seven year period. And now, in 2018, there is *Because of Love*, the book.

Because of Love is the story of Franko's life rather than the story of his art. It tells of his childhood in Italy growing up in the hands of an abusive family, in an orphanage and a children's home; his journey to London as a young man; his return to Italy many years later, as an acclaimed and accomplished artist; and of his life and his loves and his becoming an artist in between. As the writer Adrian Heathfield observed, it's "a complicated tale of redemption through art".

Franko first proposed that LADA publish his story when we showed Nathaniel's *Because of Love* film in our LADA Screens series in 2016. We, of course, leapt at the opportunity and have been working closely with him over the last year on editing his texts in ways that were true to Franko's style and voice, while assembling the other elements of this book and working with designer David Caines.

As well as Franko's life story, *Because Of Love* includes two other stories he has written about his loves – his partner Tom and his beloved dog Beuys – and a preface by the artist and writer Tim Etchells. When Giuditta Fullone, the daughter of the Italian curator and art historian Francesca Alfano Miglietti ('FAM'), read Franko's story, she created a wonderful series of illustrations to accompany it; we are delighted to be able to include these in *Because of Love*. The book is also illustrated with short statements about Franko from a wide range of people who have been significant in his life – people who know him and his work, people he loves and respects.

Things have changed enormously since Franko was growing up in 1960s Italy and living in squats in 1980s London – children in public institutions in the 60s weren't protected as they are today, for example, and the hard drug scene in London is very different to the one Franko lived through. *Because of Love* offers a glimpse into very particular lives and times and tells the story of how Franko B survived and, perhaps, even shaped them.

PREFACE
IT APPEARS, THE STORY.
TIM ETCHELLS

Fifteen years ago, maybe more. Body painted Butoh-white and moving
under bright white light Franko B walks back and forth on a canvas catwalk
stretched the length of the Tate Modern Turbine Hall. With each step blood
falls from the cannulas in his arms, swelling for short moments as dark
drops to exit his body, then falling to the floor, delicate splatters that soak
the waiting canvas, blood, like the beginning of rain. Cameras flash from
the silent crowd all around, cutting time into instants of less than a second
but Franko steps slowly, taking time, as if taking the time itself in fact and
remaking it somehow as one piece again, going forwards always, as the
blood falling writes the steady trace of his trajectory, a marked path forming
one drop at a time – a story in blood on the floor.

And so it is with words, here, now, in Franko's text. One after the other,
inexorable, back and forth between Brescia and Milan, Biandrate, Como,
Devils Gate and Brixton. There is little by way of explanation, still less by
way of psychology. Things happen. Steps are taken. The words fall, tracing
their line. There is a lot of suffering, a lot of night-time, a lot of memory
rooted in the bodies and colours of vivid incident, sex, wonder, violence,
abuse of power and death. It appears, the story. Like blood traces. Stark,
compelling, idiomatic. Vital remainders. One has the sense, sometimes
at least, of a person caught in a spiral made from other people's choices
or behaviours. Puzzled, abused, outraged, sometimes uncomprehending,
but always somehow drawn to go on, in something like good spirits, with
resolve. Back and forth. And back and forth. And passing years. And here
and there along the route, bright temporary shelters made out of love,
desire, sex, friendship and creative acts – glimpses of great joy.

What I've long valued most about Franko's work in fact is that for all its excess or privation, for all its multiplications of pain there is always, braided in some essential relation, another thing – affirming, if ephemeral. There is a private iconography, a landscape of suffering of course – harsh words, crosses, the colours of blood and spilled milk, images of the body prone or abject, birds stilled in paint like thick black pitch, a constant harking to wounds, wounding and an inner suffering. But at the same time there is a true intimacy that arises from Franko's capacity for compassion and his vulnerability inside and outside the constructed frame of his art work. Back in the Turbine Hall, when seen from a distance, he could appear for a moment more as mere image than as a person – a sign or icon, spectacular, operatic – but with greater proximity his eyes, breathing and the bleeding itself all very much belied that iconic surface.

On the catwalk, getting closer, Franko's eyes meet and make direct contact with those watching him through that long walk back and forth - flickering, lively and intense indices of a complex interior one is drawn to and compelled to guess at, his breathing a rupture to the mask also, uneven in its rise and fall, faltering here and there in connection with the bleeding perhaps; you cannot tell. And the blood itself – no theatrical spurting, no Artaud scream, no ragged splattering in rage – just a soft measure of time beaten out by the clock of the heartbeat, strong and fragile in its way, drop by drop pushing out, out and down, appearing as lines on the floor. Like words here, in the text, on the page.

Back in the early 2000s, when I was in a London hospital and very sick for a while post heart-operation, Franko was pretty much a daily visitor, his appearance itself something of a sensation on the cardiac ward where his sprawling intricacy of tattoos, laughter, gold teeth, piercings and enthusiastic talk about projects lay well outside the more-or-less normative comings and goings of aged triple-bypass and stent patients, worried spouses, handbags and Get Well Soon cards. Franko would bring Lychee juice or Portuguese cakes, once bringing Ron Athey by also to say hi, doubling down on the performative impact of Franko's own arrival. It was certainly something to wake up wired to heart monitors, drips and blood pressure devices in the Cardiac Care Unit, coming round to see Franko there. In some ways it felt like a distorted and extended reversal of a performance in which he had lain prone and wounded on the floor of a gallery, to greet lone visitors for a strictly limited and intimate appointment of exactly two minutes. I saw the piece at Toynbee Studios, must have been in 1999, and its two minutes stay with me as a paradigm of how open and how opening performance can be – a piece of framed time, charged by action, in which anything can happen. The scene's reversal in the hospital – my switch from visitor to visited, from well to sick or wounded – also made something else clear for me, echoed in Franko's writing – that the capacity for empathy enacted and activated in his work operates in some kind of mirror or exchange relation to his own experience of abjection.

In the ongoing storm of creative work that has in a sense both been Franko B's life and saved it, Franko has long known and cultivated the power of the stark image posed as art in public, the gesture left blank, remaining through insistence as problem and question, creating a unique body of arresting images, actions and sculptures, whose very simplicity often engenders their complexity. Here, in his text, he employs a related tack, as events and images are summoned in blunt quotidian outline, or as single vivid details which leave the reader wondering, imagining, alone, without such salve or closure that explanation or further detail might bring. It's a truly bewildering journey, brutal at times both as life and as punk literature – a back and forth from orphanage to abusive family home, to squat, to rave, club scene, AIDS activism, political protest and art practice – a trail that manages to be alien and yet somehow entirely recognisable. And Franko's act meanwhile - of setting it all out in words here - is a grounding gesture, generous and generative, that marks his difference and at the same time summons the reader to proximity, mutuality and community.

Reading the text you are connected to Franko – to the trace lines of what happened between Milan and London, to the route he has walked and to the strength, passion and human force of his survival in and through an extraordinary life and art practice, a life work. It's also a reminder of the political resistance inherent in his work, a resistance that has long valued human connection and insisted on the significance of empathy in a hostile social and political context. Finally perhaps the text exemplifies the ongoing achievement of Franko's work in its framing his own struggles, experiences and inspirations as deep provocations and vital invitations to the rest of us.

FOREWORD
FRANKO B

Around 2011, I started this process as I wanted to try to tell my story, or more like try to make sense of what my story was, or what I thought it was. An artist, Nina, kindly offered to help in exchange for some tutorials from me and I dictated to Nina in my flat in London over a few weeks. When I began from the very start of my memory bank, I just talked and talked with no filters and Nina wrote and wrote. And eventually we had arrived to the actual moment we were in, which was 2011. I read it once and showed it to some friends or people that expressed an interest in maybe getting it printed somehow... but nothing come of it, which I'm actually relieved about.

Sometime in 2016, I showed it to my friend Maurizio Coccia in Italy and a few months later he told me that I should get it printed. So after over 5 years of not reading it or updating it, I read it properly for the first time again and again. I decided that many of the adjectives and sentences were not in my voice or I dint any longer recognise as mine, so I re-wrote them and also edited where I thought it was necessary without wanting to embarrass people I care about. Also there were cases of things / details that I dint recall the first time or things that got mixed up and needed re-addressing. At first I thought that I dint want to have fictitious names so I could talk about people's secrets or things that were very personal and intimate for me, but on the advice of a lawyer and thinking about people's privacy I decided to change some people's names.

Also I decided not to list every time I may have taken drugs or had sex with someone, or loved or hated someone, or wanted to kill myself. I just wanted to keep this way of telling my story essentially simple and honest and without vengeance or being gratuitously nasty about someone just because they suddenly dint love me anymore or left me or I left them, or they dint help me or give me support. There have been a lot of people and things and places that I loved and hated and it will probably keep happening. But for sure I will always love my 'family', whoever that might be, in time and space and art.

In late 2016 I did the first screening of a documentary about me that Nathanial Walters had been working on for the last 6/7 years, also titled *Because of Love*. The screening was part of the Live Art Development Agency's LADA Screens series, and after the event, I decided to ask LADA if they would be interested in publishing my memoir. They immediately said yes and this collaboration was born.

I'm so happy to have worked with Lois Keidan of LADA as my editor, as we go back 22 years or so (everybody that knows me knows this is my favourite number and if you don't know why, you will by the end of reading this book).

I'm so grateful to Lois, Tim Etchells, Dominic Johnson, Adrian Heathfield, Francesca Alfano Miglietti (FAM), Cesare Fullone and Maurizio Coccia for telling me to do this, to the many people that have being so kind and helpful in this project, and to everyone that has contributed a little thought about me or how they see me or know me.

Thank you to them from the bottom of my heart, and last but not least a big thank you to Giuditta Fullone for the amazing illustrations she has made of my life story.

BECAUSE OF LOVE

Vittoria (my mother) was the last of 5 or 6 children. If I'm right she was born in Gardone Val Trompia in the province of Brescia in the north of Italy in 1939. Her parents died when she was just 5 years old. Since nobody could take care of her, she was brought up by nuns. I don't know much more about her childhood, but apparently my mother had already many emotional and mental issues.

In 1959 my mother met my father who was in the army and as a result of their short love story and fuck my mother got pregnant and I was born, but my father could not stick around for me to come out of my mother's belly. Yes it was the belly; she had to have a C section.

Much has been told about my absent father, the most credible story is that he wanted to undertake a military career (probably as a 'Carabiniere', an Italian type of police force attached to the army corps and not the state police, who tend to deal more with local domestic crime issues) which in those years meant he had to renounce, until the age of 28, any legal bond like a marriage or a child and therefore could not father any child before marriage. This was Italy in 1959, and therefore, as a result of my mother's pregnancy, my father asked to be transferred to another post in the army, and was transferred without any possible way for my mother to find him again, and as she was not married to him the army dint have to inform her about his whereabouts (this information I eventually got from my Auntie Domenica, my mother's older sister.)

I was born in Milan in 1960.

Gardone Val Trompia was a small town then, at that time it was very parochial, typical of most towns in Italy at that time, and probably still is. My expectant mother was the town scandal and people would not forget or forgive her. In those years even the word abortion was unthinkable, never mind doing it. It was totally illegal and only rich and well connected people could have afforded to have it done privately and discretely. If you were poor it was impossible. All these reasons, or perhaps the shame, drove my mother to leave Gardone Val Trompia and go to Milan. Once there, she found a job as a housekeeper somewhere.

So on the 27 January 1960 I was born at the Hospital Maggiore in Milan. I actually never lived in Milan, but somehow I ended up in an orphanage in Brescia. As my mother could not have taken care of me and herself at the same time she parked me there. Probably it was for 'technical & legal' reasons that I ended up in Brescia.

My first memory is when I was about 5 years old, during my stay at the orphanage which was run by priests. I remember very clearly one of the priests punished me for peeing while I was asleep in bed. I remember that he was angry at me, so to teach me a lesson he brought me in the toilet area of the orphanage and he hoisted me on a small partition wall of the toilet room, saying that I should stay there until I have learnt where to pee. I remember some other kids coming in the toilet area and taunting me. I don't really know or could say how long I was there before eventually someone come to take me down from the wall, as I was too small and afraid to jump off it.

My second memory is from when I was still at this orphanage at around 6 years old. I remember how one day an 'uncle' come to visit me. I dint know what an uncle was; nevertheless I remember that the uncle was a man, he seemed tall, he was wearing a military uniform, and that we spent a length of time in the backyard. In retrospect, I believe that was the first and last time I possibly seen my father. Maybe this is one of my many fantasies.

'Uncle' apart, I also had 'grandparents'. They weren't my real grandparents as I learnt later on, but they were a wealthy elderly couple from Brescia that would come to the orphanage and take care of me once in a while, and maybe also other kids. 'Grandparents' would come during the weekend and would take me to their home and I would sleep in their bed. I seem to have been happy then. A long time after, once grown up, I found out that they wanted to adopt me, but my mother never gave them the permission to do so. Also I found out that others including members of my mother's immediate family wanted to adopt me but she never give her consent.

One of the worst memories I have is the last memory of the orphanage and is when one day on my way back from school, I was 7 at that time, the person in charge of the orphanage told me that my mother had come to pick me up and take me home for good. I dint have a memory of her and I dint have any

bond with her as I dint know of her or about her existence or what the word mother meant - nobody ever told me up to then.

I remember I was sitting not far from a frosted glass door; then I seen a shadow behind moving forward. The shadow come in the room I was sitting in. This shadow was a woman, the woman was my mother. This is the first memory I have of her.

The pain was heart-rending. No more friends, no more grandparents or uncles whatsoever. I remember I felt powerless and that my opinion wouldn't be taken into consideration.

When my mother and I left the orphanage in Brescia, I wasn't aware yet that that trip to San Nazzaro Sesia, where my mother was living, was the beginning of all my trouble. San Nazzaro Sesia, in the province of Novara, in the region of Piedmont in northern Italy, was then a small town. I just remember a central community square and the municipal main building with a clock tower. During my stay at the orphanage I barely had any contact with the outside world, apart from visiting the 'grandparents'. Once at 'home' I found out that another child was living there. It was a 3 year old girl. Her name was Maria C, and she was my stepsister (at first I dint realise but later she displayed the same emotional and mental issues as my mother).

During the period I spent in the orphanage, my mother got married to Atilio and he become my stepfather and had another child which was Maria C. The funny thing is, if we want to use this term, was that my stepfather knew about my existence only after my mother and he got married in 1963 (and he wouldn't lose the chance to repeat this to me every time we would have an argument, or he was beating me up).

It was only when I was 18 that I found out why my mother came to get me from the orphanage when I was 7 years old - Auntie Domenica had convinced my mother to come to the orphanage and take care of me, as my mother being legally married made her immune from shame. My stepfather was about 13 years older than my mother. At that time, he was working night shifts in a cardboard factory in Biandrate. I also find out that he had also some mental issues, like my mother.

Once settled down I started to go to school. At that time I was in my first year class and there were around 12 children. I would sit next to the teacher's table, probably because I was new or 'special'. One day I remember the teacher asked us to do a drawing. Once I finished my drawing – which was of a boy pissing, probably a self-portrait drawn as a stick with the colour red pencil – I showed it to her. For some unknown reason she got really mad at me. She kicked me out of the room, forced me to stand still with my face facing the wall until my mother would come to pick me up.

Once at home, my mother also slapped me a few times while shouting at me, then she sent me to bed without dinner as punishment. That was the first time my mother nominated my real father with the same adjective as me, 'sei un disgrazziato come tuo padre' – *you are a disgrace, like your father* – or something like this.

From then on, every time I wasn't behaving in the way my mother wanted me to, or just when she was in a bad mood, or when her frustrations were reaching the peak, she would compare me with my father. She would say that I was a bastard like him, and I was as selfish as he was and that she could not trust me as she made an error with him. I realised how strong the bitterness my mother had towards my father was and how my presence, to my misfortune, was a bridge with her past.

Moreover I quickly learnt to not to ask my mother who my father was. Her hate towards him was so strong and deep-rooted regardless of anybody or anything. As a consequence the chance for me, one day, to know my father was zero. This is because, I believe, my mother wanted to punish him, more than me, by denying me to him.

As I said before, my mother got married, therefore my stepfather become my legal father as at that time in Italian law a man who married a woman that had already a child had to legally adopt this child even if he dint know the existence of such a child (as my stepfather always claimed). I believe that on a winter day in '67 or early 68' I was legally given my father's surname in front of the mayor of the town of San Nazzaro Sesia (who happened to be the husband of the teacher that was mad at me for the 'rude' child drawing).

More or less in the same period I remember I received a letter. It was a letter from my (fake) grandparents who used to pick me up at the orphanage.

I can't recall what the letter was saying, maybe because I was not good at reading, yet I remember that apart from the letter there was a 10,000 lira note (a good amount of money in those years) as a present for me. I remember the money not because I am a greedy bastard, but because my mother made me write to the grandparents in order to ask them for more money. I never heard from them anymore.

Biandrate was 3 to 5 kilometres from San Nazzaro Sesia. I can't remember the reason why one day we moved from San Nazzaro Sesia to Biandrate. We moved into the third floor of a three-storey building. The flat was very humble, with one bedroom, and a sitting room and kitchen as one. The toilet was outside the flat, in between floors near to the stairs and it was in common use with the other tenants. Soon my mother began to work for an elderly woman who was living in a manor house bordering the building we were living in (maybe she was even our landlady).

Soon I discovered that my stepfather's relatives were not aware of my existence. My stepfather had hidden the fact that his wife had a child with another man before his marriage with her as it would have been seen as a scandal.

As a matter of fact, one Sunday one of my stepfather's brothers come to Biandrate to visit my mother, my stepfather and Maria C. So I was hidden under the main bed in the bedroom. I stayed there around the time of the visit, and I still remember how, at a certain point I seen two children that were looking at me. My sister had brought them there not understanding what she was doing while the adults got distracted. I dint feel relief at all, as long as I remember, mostly because I had the certainty that it wasn't a game of hide and seek, I would not be able to jump out from under the bed and scream 'TAAAADAA you've found me!!!'

Once the children left the bedroom I would hear their excited voices telling their parents that a child was hiding under the bed. My mother promptly ran towards the door, and while she was shutting it, she would say that children have such a fervent imagination to make them see children under beds. (It must have been weird for the children that actually did see me and probably this image stayed with them for long time , and I cannot imagine the conversation in their car on their way home).

In the autumn of 1968 I began to go to school occasionally in the new town of Biandrate and in November of that year my mother disappeared for a while. I can't remember how long as I hadn't developed an awareness about time, but I remember my sister and I were alone at home most of the day. We would have canned beef and canned tuna and bread, and I wouldn't go to school as I was babysitting Maria C.

Eventually my mother come back. I believe she had a caesarean like she did to have me as she was holding two little babies in her arms – twins Monica and Luisella. I dint even realise that my mother was pregnant and it was never mentioned to me or talked about it, maybe because I dint even know what a pregnancy was.

Straight after her return home my mother started working again. As I had now to take of my 3 younger sisters, the time I was allowed to go to school become less and less. Twice a week I would wake up very early in the morning, go to the municipal offices of Biandrate to collect milk vouchers, and then walk for about 2 kilometres to the nearest farm to collect fresh milk with a tin milk container. I remember I would pass by the factory where my stepfather was working, a massive cardboard packaging factory.

Doing shopping was also part of my daily and weekly duties: shopping included asking for credit to the shopkeeper, telling them that my mother will pass by and pay for the goods at end of the month when my stepfather got paid and going to the priest of the only church of the town, sometimes to our neighbours, other times all over the town to beg for money from people I dint even know. Of course this was a lot of stress for me as I was only 8 or 9 years old and my mother would physically attack me if I failed to come home with the goods. When I failed I would try to get her to promise me that she would not beat me up if I agreed to enter the house again.

By the time I was 9 years old I was able to cook mashed potatoes and rice and pasta soup for my sisters.

Sometimes, when my mother was at work, and I was at home looking after my sisters and cleaning the house, I remember how naively I would put the clock back. I was quite sure that in this way, she wouldn't notice if I wasn't able to finish all the duties she had asked me to do but of course she did notice it.

In the second floor of the building, right next to the stairs, there was a flat occupied by an old woman. Just outside the flat, and right under the stairs there was a small nook where the woman would keep different things.

At that time, living with my mother and family become more and more uncomfortable. With the excuse to go to the toilet, I would go straight to the small nook and eat what I was able to keep from the shopping, usually bread. The woman realised what was going on and that I was using her nook but nevertheless she kept the secret and never said a word to my family, in fact she sympathised with me.

My stepfather was employed at the cardboard factory and he was working most night shifts, but I dint remember him being around that much somehow. All of us were sleeping in a single room. I was sleeping in a single bed, Maria C in another tiny bed, and mother and the twins in her large one with my stepfather when he was home. Sometimes my stepfather was coming back in the middle of the night and going straight to bed, though if my mother was convinced I did not behave properly, she would have left him a message explaining how bad I was and that I needed his attention. Which would had been to wake me up and beat me with his belt.

Soon I started to become terrorised as I was never able to know or understand when my mother was going to write a message to my stepfather. I just remember that she was writing them quite often. I was frightened of my stepfather and of the dark. Even now, wherever I may be I need a small light in the room or corridor during night-time, especially if its somewhere not familiar.

The only trips I remember, which I did occasionally with my mother, were to Novara, the nearest city to where we lived and to Auntie Domenica's house back in San Nazzaro Sesia.

I remember the occasion of one trip to Novara with my mother. We went by coach and went to a supermarket which was part of a chain called Upim or sometime also to another supermarket called Standa – very similar to Marks & Spencer and Tesco but Italian-style. My mother bought me a new shirt. I remember it was beige with a repetition of patterns all over. I think that I liked it, but I can't remember, though during the trip back my mother and I started to have an argument or disagreement. The only thing I remember is that, as soon as we reached home, she took my new shirt, and she cut it into pieces and then she threw it into the fire stove.

As Auntie Domenica was living not too far from us, we tended to see her more than anybody else of our extended blood family. Her husband / my uncle was called Aldo and was a builder, and I remember he was an alpha male who always seemed to express that he was the boss in the house, and I had the impression that he was always looking down on my mother and I. I remember that he liked to hunt or shoot anything that moved, especially in the air. Domenica and Aldo had a son called Moreno and a daughter called Mariangela. Moreno was 6 or 7 years older than me.

Once while I was there and my mother was busy talking with Auntie Domenica, Moreno gave me some wine. I remember how he was laughing at me as I was completely drunk. I also remember how after a while I felt sick and threw up in the kitchen sink. When Auntie Domenica and my mother realised that I was drunk, they were not impressed and we got into trouble.

When I think of those days in San Nazzaro Sesia and Biandrate I wouldn't say that school was something that I was used to, although I have a faint memory of going to school when I was at the orphanage, but I dint go often because I started my school later than other kids. Because of my birthday being in January I started elementary school when I was nearly 7 years old and then my mother arrived on to the scene which meant I was over a year behind in respect to other children that had earlier birthdays.

So when I was in Biandrate going to school seemed so sporadic that I have only got few memories of it. I do remember going briefly to an old school that was then demolished because it was so old and dangerous. So the council built another school which wasn't far from where the old school stood. Weirdly enough I used to see into my old classroom from the flat we were living in. I also remember in the new school how once, during a lesson, I peed myself. I peed myself because of fear of putting my hand up to ask for permission in front of all the others kids and to ask to go to toilet.

I by now felt like an outsider and that I dint belong. I knew somehow that my family and I were not considered 'normal'. I think that I had developed an inferiority complex. The town was talking about us – about the screaming from the house, when my mother and stepdad had a fight over some things, like the lack of money or me, the asking for credit, the door-to-door begging, going to the priest to ask for money, not being sent to school regularly, the beating and the bruising on me, the smell of piss on me.

It was a small town but having said this we were not the only troubled family in Biandrate. For sure we were not the only white trash family there.

I can recall now there was a child called Fernando. His family was very large and was also really poor and his big brothers were often in trouble for stealing and violence and in prison for this. They were from the south of Italy – I don't remember where exactly – but in the 60s and 70s there was a lot of intolerance towards people from the south from the people of the north of Italy and even I was called names by other kids and adults in reference to this (although my mother or I were not from the south). The most used word to show dislike for you would be 'terrone' or in dialect 'terron'.

Once Fernando called me from the street below (I was 3 floors up and my mother was not in the house). He was with some of his brothers. I looked out of the window and he asked me for some money and when I replied that I did not have any he suggested I look into my mother's bag, so stupidly I did – I don't know why but I did. I would climb a chair in order to reach my mother's bag and throw to Fernando what I found.

That was perhaps the only time I could remember that my mother punished me rightly. Though... I think that I dint know and understand the value of the money that somehow he bullied me into giving to him.

Later on when my mother come home and I told her what happened she dint believe that I had just given it to some kids that asked or bullied or tricked me into giving our only money away to them. She would ask me where the money really went and I would reply that I did not have it and that Fernando asked me to give it to him. Eventually she believed me and told me to go to Fernando house and to ask for the money back, so I did as I dint have any choice in the matter, but she dint come with me and it was to no avail.

When I asked Fernando and his brothers for the money back they looked at me like I was mad. I got a good beating from my mother and my stepfather when he found out about it. I must have been 9 years old.

At the beginning of this story I described my mother as having some mental illness issues and also my stepfather, and eventually also my stepsister Maria C did develop serious mental instability. They all had some sort of bipolar and autism.

When my mother got upset about something she would get in a real distress state which usually meant pulling her hair and hitting herself and throwing the first things she would get her hands on at the wall or at anyone she was angry with in that moment of craziness. This could be anything from a bottle of cooking oil to a pair of scissors.

When she was having a raging fit, I knew that in this moment I needed to get out of the house and run downstairs otherwise I would get hurt, then she would go to the window and start to shout at me 'Where are you? Disgrace! Come back home!' and I would be on the street asking her to promise she would not beat me up. This would happen often when there was a drama, never mind how big or small it may be.

My stepfather was never at home and when he was it was not good news for all of us but usually I would get the brunt of it. The neighbours or people passing by could not avoid seeing or hearing what was going on. It was free dramas for them, and there was always some kind of free dramas for sure.

It was summer time, and one evening my mother and I went for a walk with my 3 little sisters around the town. Maria C would have been nearly 6 and the 2 twins Luisella and Monica would have been about 9 or 10 months maximum. They were in a double buggy pushed by my mother and Maria C would have been walking with us. Once back at home mother realised that one of the twins had lost her little shoe.

We were poor and we could not afford to buy new shoes for them so my mother was not happy and started to have a raging fit like it was my fault. She sent me out to the now dark night to find the shoe. I remember that I walked all the way back, it was already dark, and I couldn't find the shoe. For some reason my mother blamed me.

One of the twins, Luisella, had problems learning to walk. I seem to remember that she was not strong enough to stand up or walk on her own. My mother and I would go with her to a specialist once a month for a while to a clinic based in the city of Novara. The specialist gave her a diet based on calcium and some injection. Eventually later on, at the age of over three, she would be able to stand on her own legs and start to walk.

Another recurrent memory is the feelings of the dark and loneliness while I was living with my mother and family. I think I was about 10 years old by now and my life was super stressful and I was not going to school any more. Really, something had happened and I don't know why but one night I started touching my genitals in my bed in our dark bedroom that I was sleeping with the rest of the family. I started feeling comfort and some kind of body warmth. (Basically in a weird kind of way I started masturbating but I dint know at this time what this was.) The more I was touching it, the more I had pleasure... I guess that it was more than a sexual pleasure, as I dint know what sexual pleasure was – it was also a feeling of self-consolation. At that time I dint know what an orgasm was, yet while I was there, laying on my bed basically unknowingly masturbating myself, I thought I was seeing the Virgin Mary in that dark lonely cold room. Perhaps it was a mystical vision... I remember that the next night I tried it again... but I never seen her again.

My mother somehow eventually noticed as we were in the same room although in total darkness, that during the nights I was touching myself, and she come to me and pulled the blanket out of my bed and turned the light on and said that I was too young to do such a thing as I was still a child. Moreover she told my stepfather what I had been doing. The next night I was motionless, frightened in my bed. I was waiting and waiting for my stepfather to come home and beat me up. Eventually he came, but he did not touch me.

The following day my mother reminded my stepfather about my new habit while we were having lunch or something like that. I remember his

expression when he turned his face, he looked at me and the only thing I remember was his look of disgust but I think also maybe he felt sorry for me for the first time.

Even though I don't recall any positive memory of the 3 years I spent with my mother after she came to get me at the orphanage in 1967 to September 1970, which was when I was sent to a boarding institution run by the Italian Red Cross, sometimes when my mother was happy she would make delicious apple pies and tomato sauces and once she took me to the cinema as a present for my first Communion. I can't remember much of the movie, so I guess that it was more a present for her than for me – Doctor Zhivago was certainly not for kids of my age. Omar Sharif was starring in it, who my mother was a big fan of, and the only memories I have of this film was the blood and violence and that it was about the 1917 Russian Revolution with a Hollywood treatment and Omar Sharif. I remember my mother loved Omar Sharif.

One night, the sergeant from the local police station of Biandrate (Carabinieri) come to our house. My stepfather was at home, maybe he was told to be present. Maybe it was because of school or not school? Maybe it was the free theatre that my family was producing more and more for the benefits of the town? The few times I had the chance to go to school I would be sent dirty and scruffy and smelling of my own piss, and after a while the school and the people of Biandrate had noticed it and someone decided to make a complaint to the police. I guess that the reason why the sergeant come around that night wasn't because he cared about the fact I was continuously abused mentally and physically, more for the fact that my family wasn't able to do it without making any noise. They should have learnt that the dirty washing has to be laundered at home. This was my interpretation of the facts after witnessing the police representative.

After about a few months of the visit by the police sergeant, the friendly advice that he gave to my family must not have worked or it was too late anyway and it become a real legal issue. My family had carried on abusing me and not sending me to school, until receiving a letter.

The letter was from the Magistrate office of Brescia which was ordering my mother to bring me to a paediatrics centre in the city of Novara, for a physiological and physiological assessment I believe. This took a few visits while the doctors would try to understand if I was 'normal' or somehow traumatised by circumstances in my life and if this had affected my cognitive growth.

The only thing I remember at this clinic is that I had to draw a lot and they would ask me questions and made me play with some toys in their clinic and made me play with other kids while they were observing me. I don't know for how long I went there but once I remember they stuck some paste to my hair and attached some wires to my scalp with some padded senses. The wires were attached to a big machine that was responding by drawing some graphic lines and made weird noises (it was like something out of Frankenstein movies) and the only thing I know is that the results of this test established that my brain was 'working' and the problem and slow development was very likely a product of my family and domestic environment.

It was established that I was not lying when they asked me what it was like living with my family, which of course my mother was not happy about. Therefore in order to protect the development of my social inclusion I shouldn't live anymore with my family and I needed special care and schooling away from them. Then they explained the normal local school was not equipped to deal with pupils like me (today I would probably have been considered a child with a learning difficulty for whatever reason).

What happened next was very stressful.

My mother and me were summoned by the Magistrate of the city of Brescia to answer some questions, and I remember that I was taken in a room with some people alone and my mother was told to stay outside but the wall of the room was only half to the ceiling and my mother would hear what I would say so I was shit scared and I dint answer the questions they were asking me, or dint answer truthfully because I was scared of reprisal from my mother.

Nobody explained or told me what was going on, my mother had to answer some questions in front of a judge and at the end he decided to fine her 400,000 lira which was a lot of money for my mother and family to pay back then in 1969. Needless to say my mother was not happy and took it out on me on the coach and once back at home.

I don't know who or what institution or authority decided to refer me to a Pedagogical Institute of the Italian Red Cross based on the lake of Mergozzo, as I was from that moment on ward under protection of the Italian state (social services). The institute provided me with the continuation of my education. I was 10 years old and 8 months and I was still in the second elementary year. In 3 years I had progressed from first elementary to second elementary. Consider that in normal circumstances a 10 year old is in fifth class.

Also at the institute and new boarding school I would be followed by psychologists and paediatricians that would help me to cope with my emotional and psychological traumas. This was what the institute did not just for me but for almost 90 kids, but more importantly for me it protected me from my parents. Nevertheless, the centre was for reintegrating children in post-domestic-conflict situations into society through rehabilitation and educative programmes and it did that with what I would call basic schooling and the kind of moral teaching and indoctrination found in Italy of that time.

I was obligated to keep contact with my mother throughout my time at the institute through visits and by post although she personally never wrote or answered the letters I had to write home or even visited me in the 4 years I was at this boarding school.

It must have been late August or early September 1970, I was 10 years and 8 months old. It was the end of summer and my mother accompanied me to my 'new home' at the institute. We travelled from Biandrate. The lake of Mergozzo which also was under the province of the city of Novara was not that far from the Swiss Alps. The journey looked to me to be endless, I felt sick and we had to stop a few times as I vomited. Where we were going could not have been actually that far, maybe 2 hours.

The first memory I recall of Mergozzo is the town square full of many stands of freshly caught fish, then an enormous tree with a hole so huge that I could see the lake through it. It was not a large lake by any means and it was part of a succession of lakes (the lake Maggiore and the lake of D'Orta were larger lakes than the Mergozzo one). There was lot of people at the lakefront that day I arrived in Mergozzo, probably because it was one of the last warm days of summer. A bit further up, on a hill there was a large mansion with a huge red cross painted on its out face looking onto the lake. I believe it was built in the 1800s and used to belong to a French Count that donated it to the Italian Red Cross.

At the entrance of the wall that marked the boundary of the property there was a marble plate with 'Pedagogic Institute Fauser Gajetti' written on it. The mansion was arranged over three floors with a long driveway and was so big that it was easy to see it from the centre of the village and the painted red cross on a square white back ground did give a specific identity to the place.

At the entrance there were many children and adults. I was a bit intimidated or shy, though at the same time curious. I was happy to be there. It was a Sunday late afternoon, my mother left me to someone and after some paperwork she left.

The first thing I did, with the rest of the children and institute's assistants, was to go out of the mansion and explore the surroundings. There was a vast pine wood and many meadows. We wandered for a while then once back inside the institute dinner was served and we were shown where to sleep.

The dormitory was a large room with many single beds. I wasn't scared to be there, I dint miss home, and actually I was excited, I also felt safe with all those other children that in some way inevitably were sharing my own fate. But most importantly I wasn't with my mother and the rest of my family.

The day after, we were inspected by the nuns to be sure that we, the new children, did not have any lice and fleas. They undressed us one by one, washed us in a big bath and after they sprinkled us with some disinfectant powder.

During the inspection the nuns weighed me up. Apparently my weight was far below the average of a nearly 11 year old child. My weight was under 40 kg. I remember that one of the nuns that was checking me noticed bruises and scars on my back and she asked me how I got them.

Apart from the 3 nuns that were in charge of the domestic side of things, like cleaning, cooking, gardening, laundry and basic medical care, the

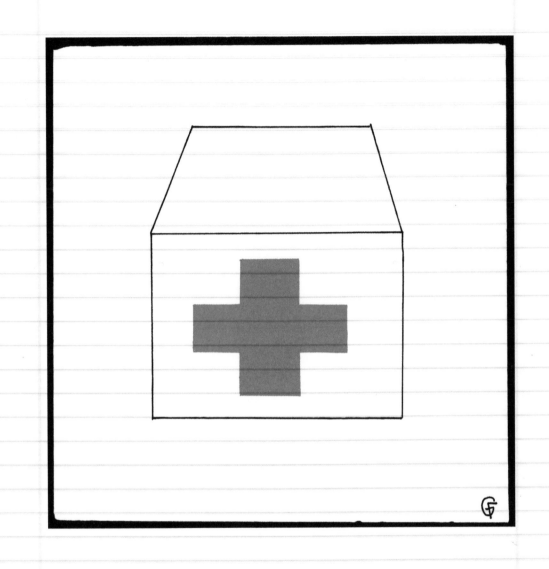

rest of the staff were civil servants like the teachers, the director and the professionals that occasionally interacted with the kids and the assistants that took care of the kids out of school lesson time.

Every child had a number: my number was 22 for the entire time I spent at the institute. The uniform consisted of a blue jumper and a pair of grey shorts with your personal number sewn inside. I remember how I had to mend my own stockings and pants sometimes as I got a bit older.

A new routine I had was to brush my teeth twice a day, this was new to me.

The refectory was a very big circular room, in the middle of which the cart of food was placed. The nuns were in charge of serving, and if any food was left one could ask for a second helping. Usually at lunch there was pasta, meat or mashed potatoes – on Friday breaded fish, on Sunday chicken. At dinner, soups, cheese or vegetables. Every assistant had her children sit at 2-3 large round tables, while the director had her own table in the centre. She was usually eating with us during lunchtime. She was from the city of Ferrara and as long as I remember she was ok.

The mansion had many rooms. The laundry and the kitchen were on the ground floor, while the classes on the first. The third was dedicated to the dormitory. Nuns and assistants would sleep in 2 other separate small buildings outside the mansion. When not on duty there was also a small church, a small yard that was used as a football pitch, but with no grass, and a small outdoor swimming pool and a gym that we would use once a week after school.

Sometimes we would go fishing to the lake that was basically in front of our institute with only the main road separating it. The lake was surrounded by a variety of trees and camping sites. My favourite though was the willow tree. The institute grounds had a water stream coming down from the mountains behind that went under the road straight into the lake. We would use bamboo rods that we would find along the lake to fish. I remember once I fished a few tiny fish. But another time, while I was walking back to the institute after a walk, I found a dead fish. The eyes of that fish were wide open. I was so convinced that the fish was staring at me that since then I stopped eating fish or fishing it.

Soon after arriving at the Red Cross I started going to school. I was in my second year, I was ten, and the teacher was good and nice. All the teaching staff where generally pleasant. When not in class we were looked after by the assistants that were usually girls and women between 19 and 25 years old who were doing their training to become teachers or social workers. Altogether there were 6-8 assistants and each of them had her own group composed of 10-15 children that varied from the second to the fifth year.

Overall the assistants were civil and professional, with the exception of 2 of them that I will remember for the rest of my life but for the wrong reasons. Their names were Beata and Olivia and I could not tell you which one was more sadist than the other; they where so inept and uninterested in the wellbeing of their charges, they should not have been in the position they were, never mind working with children.

I was lucky enough that the assistant I had in the first 2 years was very good and she treated me like I was her own son or younger brother. Her name was Raffaella and she was from a small town called Ornavasso. She was pretty and with a good taste in dressing, and she had long beautiful hair. I was a small boy so to me she seemed tall and would wear a very long coat. She would sing loud – often songs by pop stars of that time like Lucio Battisti and a group called Pooh.

Unfortunately when Raffaella would have her day off, sometimes I would have to be under the supervision of sadist Beata or Olivia and I would often witness them abusing their position with the children they were looking after. For example if you had done something they dint like they would punish you – make you kneel on small pebbles while holding your arms up or castigating you by putting you beyond where the television in the TV room was on during kids programmes like cartoons and films, so you could hear it but could not see it. Or standing in the courtyard for 3 hours without moving because you asked if you could go to the toilet when according to them you should not have, or talking to another kid at the dinner table. There were no warnings of any kind that you had done something wrong, you just got their designated punishment when you dint expect it. Basically they were bullies, both of them. They were the only ones who would beat you even for a tiny silly thing, like talking to yourself, and even if you were not at fault.

My first experience of Olivia's sadistic streak was when I was 12 years old and Raffaella was on her day off and I happened to be under the supervision of Olivia for that day. That day in the evening, after classes, I was in the corridor just outside the TV room with some other kids talking and playing and for some reason Olivia come out of the room and just slapped me hard as she could, so I asked what it was for and she slapped me again and again and again and also started to pull my hair till I stopped asking that question and admitted that I knew what it was for. Eventually I had to admit that I knew what I did wrong even if I dint know and she dint tell me what it was. After this I hoped I never had to be in her care or in the group of kids she was in charge of.

The thing is that Beata and Olivia had a bad reputation with other members of staff that worked in the institute in different areas, not just the kids. They should have been incompatible to work in a such a place. As I said before, in the institute most of the children had different, let's say, 'personal' issues and problems. Sometimes these problems would have been expressed as a physical and biological reaction. Some children were very violent, others would piss their own beds most nights and some in their trousers in the day. As for myself I wet the bed very often at the very beginning of my stay at the Red Cross. With the passing of time it become less and less frequent and I did eventually only occasionally wet the bed, which I did till I was 16 years old.

There were other children with bleeding noses, and I remember in particular a child that we would call Giuseppino who would shit in his trousers most days. Giuseppino was 2-3 years younger than me and although in Raffaella's care when not in the classroom, definitely not in my class. Once, after the second or third time he shit in his trousers, I remember noticing that Raffaella was not coping well with Giuseppino so I offered to take him to the toilet area and help him to wash and dress him up with clean clothes. To me he was like a small brother. I was used to this with my small stepsisters back at home. I dint have any problem with it and I ended up doing it a few times when it was necessary.

Suddenly, I don't know what had happened to him, but I dint see him anymore.

That year the group that Raffaella had in her charge was definitely younger and I should have not been in her group but when they try to put me with another assistant and group I cried and I was allowed to stay under her charge for another year. Raffaella had developed a particular interest in me as a child, also for the reason that she was studying psychology at the university of Cattolica in Milan, to then to become a teacher, which she did and left the Red Cross to teach eventually in the town she came from. She told me 40 years later I was her case study for her final exams. To me she became like the bigger sister I never had. When we went to walk with the rest of the group when we were not in class, we were holding hands all the time. I was always next to her.

Raffaella was living in a small town not far from the institute but a good walk away and sometimes, especially at weekend, she would take her group of kids to her house to meet her parents and see where she lived. The only problem was that to reach Raffaella's house we had to cross a primitive wooden bridge. The bridge was old, moving and with a hole in the centre and it was very high above a large river. Raffaella, maybe because she was used to it, would have crossed it in few fast steps, but for us, every time was a terrifying experience. I found out there that I suffer with vertigo. The bridge must have been built by the partisans during the second world war I thought.

When I started my fourth year of primary school Raffaella left the Red Cross. Nevertheless she continued to come and visit me.

During my 4 years' stay at the Red Cross Institute I was still wetting my bed although gradually less and less. I remember the nuns tried to give me all sorts of remedy, such as some red colour pills to retain water, or not allowing me to drink water at dinnertime. But it dint work all the time. Often I would dream I would go to the loo and wee in the proper toilet but I was doing it in the bed instead. Sometimes I would be laughed at by some of the other children. Then the cleaner changed the sheets, but because we weren't allowed to have a shower in the morning on our own, most of the time I would stink of piss.

While in the Red Cross I found out I was suffering from sleepwalking and would also talk while sleeping. The second bad experience I had with Olivia was when one night she was on night duty, usually there would be a curtained off space within the big dormitory which had a bed for the person on night duty. The morning after I got into trouble she called me and started to tell me off about me talking at night in bed and getting up to go to the toilet a few times. I told her that it was not me talking and it was better if I went to the toilet so I would not wet the bed but as a result she just slapped me saying that I shouldn't answer her back.

After this time I actively avoided her and her friend Beata in any ways possible, by volunteering the kitchen, or gardens or laundry, or attaching myself to other assistants that I liked. The good things for me actually was that for some reason neither of them looked after the older boys when not in class and thinking about it, it was probably because they dint want to, or were scared, or because it was more easy to abuse the younger kids.

During my time at the Red Cross Institute I had to see a psychologist and other professionals, but I don't remember what their role was. Usually he or she would make me draw and ask me questions. Once I remember it was a woman and she asked me why I kept drawing children running in the woods and why I was colouring all trees and sometimes people in red pencil? I remember I answered because I like the colour red but I dint really know why I did this. Maybe it was because I loved running through the woods and forest – it made me feel free when I did this.

Maybe not surprisingly during this period I started developing a dislike for authority and especially organised abusive authority in any of the forms I was becoming aware of. Especially the church and the military; I dint like conflicts, I dint like wars – any wars – I could not watch war films whatever they depicted... Cowboys and Indians, the second world war, the Christian crusade etc... etc...

I remember one day I heard from the radio some news of something happening. Although I was hearing this somehow, I could visualise what it was like that I was hearing. The news was about the military coup in Chile, how they killed President Allende who was democratically elected by the

people of Chile because he was a socialist, how they tortured and murdered people. Also I remember seeing the news on the TV about demonstrations against the war in Vietnam.

During the school breaks or the weekends and also in wintertime, the assistants would bring us for a walk, usually after lunch. We would walk a lot, for miles and miles. What I really liked about these walks was the fact that, as far I could have been away from it, I would still be able to see the Red Cross mansion with the big Red Cross emblem on its building. For me it had become a point of reference: that was my home, and I felt I belonged there. Other times though I wouldn't go for the walk, partly to avoid to be under the tutelage of assistants like Olivia or Beata or other bullies, and preferred to stay in the institute to help the domestic staff in the kitchen to tidy up, do the washing up, or I would go to help the nuns gardening or doing other chores.

I remember how in the last 2 years at the Red Cross (between 12 and half years old and 14 and half years old) I started to prefer spending my time with the adults, also because I did not have so many close friends. In my last two years at the institute I hardly played with any child. The other children did not bother me though. Just once I got into a fight with another kid more or less my age as he was trying to bully me. We had a big fight and I won and since then he did not bother me anymore.

I got on ok with the cleaners and the women that were working in the kitchen, nonetheless my favourite was Franca, the cook. Sometimes she would bring me to her house. I believe she was a lonely person and quite Catholic. She would start calling me 'the advocate, the little lawyer' as I always took the side against authority and also because I was always talking a lot.

The large service kitchen at the Red Cross was more and more the place where I felt most comfortable, and I treated it like it was mine. Sometimes I would go there without any permission. I would grab a bread roll, usually with butter and sugar on it, then I would hide in the toilet to eat it.

In my third school year a new teacher come. His name was Luigi. This was a source of hilarity as his name was reminder to most of us of a then-famous advertisement for chocolate. He seemed very puritan and was very religious and quite conservative. This was my impression but he seemed fair with us. He seemed very active in the Red Cross and also was the only male member of teaching staff. There was only one other man working there and he was the gardener. I remember him, he was a very lovely old man. Sometimes I would go to his old stone house just near the Red Cross place on the hills.

In the Red Cross garden there was also a dog. He was mixed with a German shepherd. His name was Rocky. He wouldn't bite but bark and I was scared of crossing the garden if he wasn't chained but he was ok really.

I don't know why but between my fourth and fifth year, the nuns got me to become an altar boy in the little chapel in the ground of the institute. The priest of the town of Mergozzo was also our priest and Religious Education teacher. I remember how one day in my last year at the Red Cross (and no longer an altar boy by choice) I told him I dint believe in God because I couldn't explain to myself the wars, atrocities, and poverty (I know now that this was a very simplistic way of looking at it). He got mad at me. He compared me with Saint Thomas – 'Doubting Thomas' – and then kicked me out of the class.

After two or three days the nuns of the Red Cross cornered me and said to me that if I carried on saying that I didn't believe in God I wouldn't be able to wear long legged trousers like real men do. As it happened it was the same nun that brought me to a dentist one day.

My teeth weren't in a good condition and so I would go to the dentist once a week, for at least three months. The bill was around 32,000 old Italian lira, which was a great amount of money in that period, and I remember how the nun was complaining about this fact and wondering who was going to pay for it. I guess someone from the Red Cross paid the dentist (co-incidentally the dentist in question was the uncle of Massimo, Raffaella's future husband. Later on in this story all 3 will reappear after 40 years).

Usually, during Christmas and Easter holidays, there were between 1 and 4 children that dint have a home to go to. Those children who were not going back to their families for the holidays or dint have any place to go, such as me, were sent to the charitable people of Mergozzo or the towns near the institute, or to the assistants' family houses, mostly because in this way the assistants could celebrate the festivities in their homes instead of at the Red Cross.

I spent 4 different Christmases with different assistants or local people that volunteered to look after us. I remember one assistant's house from one year. There were 3 of us children, and we slept in a king-size bed. I remember it was pretty cold and someone in the house gave us hot water bottles. One was a very old metal one, the other one was made of rubber and it was blue. I still remember nowadays the comforting and warm feelings I had on sleeping in a large bed with other children like me. But the hot water bottle reminds me of feelings of solitude and belonging nowhere.

In another year on Christmas night I was lonely, I dint have anybody and I was among strangers. They were nice strangers but still strangers.

On a funnier note, the nuns' car was a Fiat 600, and the assistants usually had the smaller Fiat 500, while I remember one of the psychiatrists had a black Porsche. I remember once, during my fifth year, I went to his office. He asked me if I would have liked to have a coffee or a cigarette and after I said yes, he would say that I was not going to have any. Perhaps he wanted to point out that I could not have everything that I desired and wanted to show that I was nobody and that he had the power to mess me around.

In that period I was becoming more and more independent and even an anarchist... I was spending most of my time between the kitchen, garden, class and around the institute most of the time not in a group. I was desperate to grow up, I wanted to be an adult – and fast – so I could do whatever I wanted to... This was for me the idea of adulthood.

Around Easter time of 1974, Luigi, then my fifth year class teacher, brought me to mother's house for the Easter break. In the car with Luigi on the way to my mother, he told me that my time at the institute was coming to an end because education-wise it was the end of the line as far they were concerned. The institute only provided primary education and I would have to be accepted to another 'special' institute to carry on with my secondary education.

I was proving to be a difficult teenager to handle and was unlikely to be passed on to another institute so Luigi, who had direct experience of dealing with me for the last 2 years, come up with this idea to try to slowly re-insert me with my 'biological' family. My thought today is that the social workers and the Red Cross had had enough of me and that I was becoming uncontrollable in many ways and also sexually more active.

Anyway I don't know if my family was aware of the fact that I was going to spend my Easter holiday with them. I remember how awful the experience was. In those 4 years at the institute in Mergozzo, my family had moved away from Biandrate (not surprising after the scandal with me) to Cascina la ca' Frazione di Lesmo, a small town near Milan. In the village there was a famous Italian meat factory owned by the Molteni family who actually lived just across from the factory and a couple of streets away from us.

I realised while I was at home for this 2 weeks' break that my mother moved there as all my stepfather's family were originally from there and living around there. But they were better off than their mentally disturbed brother and son. There were so many families of the same name in this area called Brianza, but not necessary related – they had a common family name.

I spent 2 weeks there without really believing or knowing that in three months' time I would move there with my family indefinitely. I was given a bed, in the same room where my mother and sisters were sleeping, and of course as old habits die hard, I spent my holiday taking care of my younger sisters. Now Maria C was almost 11 years old and the twins nearly 6 years old.

The day I was supposed to go back to the Red Cross, my stepfather, who was supposed to take me to the nearest train station in the town of Arcore to catch a train for Central Milan and then go back to Mergozzo, come to pick me up at the house late. I think it was a Sunday, once on our way I think

I remember seeing Franko for the first time. The images of his work are imprinted onto my eyes: bright red blood trickling down painted white skin, shimmering gold punch bag as he is boxing himself to exhaustion, or stood vulnerable and tiny next to an enormous polar bear. His work is unbearably beautiful and startlingly disturbing. But words cannot capture the feeling of being with Franko, of losing your breath, of feeling as though the earth is shaking.

Martin O'Brien, artist

Jean Genet wrote that an artist can acknowledge no authority, save that of another artist.
Franko B is a great artist. And a great friend.

Cesare Fullone, artist

that he got the wrong train station. He left me alone at a station called Porta Garibaldi. The 'lovely' man left me in the wrong station and on my own and the only thing I knew was that I had to take a train to Novara for the institute, so I asked people that were around where I needed to go.

To go to the right station I had to go under a subway and tunnels and once I was there I noticed different men loitering around and looking at me weirdly and then I noticed two men that were basically masturbating and kissing each other. I soon realised that another man was following me. He was in his 30s and he was able to touch my ass and to signal to me silently to follow him outside the station, but I did not follow him.

There was a man in his 60s, waiting for the train I guess, so I asked him if I was in the right place for the train to Mergozzo. I felt relieved when he nodded affirmatively. Eventually a train arrived and the old man told me to jump on. The train was empty and strangely there was nobody else on the platform to board this train and somehow me and the man ended up sitting in the same carriage. Again I noticed that there was nobody else around.

The man shut the door of the carriage and then forced me to suck his dick. He come in my mouth very quickly then quickly he pulled his trousers up and gave me 500 lire.

I realised that the old man tricked me but I was not upset or bothered about it. I actually liked it and just wished that he had given me more money than the 500 lire. Actually we were lucky not to get caught as a train conductor came on the train and asked what we were doing on it as the train was not going anywhere, so we got off and the old man quickly disappeared.

The train I needed was nowhere and I was certainly not where I needed to be. It was getting late and there were no more trains for the Red Cross Institute town so I caught a train back to where my mother lived and had to explain what happened, but not everything.

The following morning I restarted my journey back to the Red Cross to the relief of the nuns who were worried about my one day delay. During lunch I would tell the other kids of my same age about the old man in the train. They laughed but they probably thought that I made the story up.

Sometimes I would play table tennis in the bigger boys' playroom. One day I started fighting with my friend Riccardo who was playing with me. We had some disagreement, I don't remember exactly why. As we were playing he threw one of the table tennis rackets and hit me on the back of my head and I ended up been taken by one of the nuns to the nearest hospital, where I got four stitches in my forehead.

That was the second time I went to hospital. The first time it was at the same hospital, I think in the town of Verbania, about 15 minutes by car from the institute. I was 11 and there was something wrong in the way my chest was growing. Doctor Arancio wanted me to wear an orthopaedic corset, but after a week I was there he changed his mind, maybe because he realised that as I was still so young, my chest could recover on its own in the growing. He was right.

I also recall how I hated doing sport, or any sort of activity that required a physical attitude. The other boys would play football and do athletics; I preferred art lessons, especially in my last 2 years at the institute. I would do mosaic with paper. During the night, if I couldn't get asleep I would go to the toilet, working at the art mosaics I was doing on board with paper and glue and sometimes talking to my friend Riccardo (yes, the same Riccardo that sent me to the hospital that time).

Once the nun who had her room downstairs, directly underneath the toilet where we were talking, heard us and came up to tell us off and accused us of doing something sinful like masturbating. The next day the director, during lunchtime in the dining room in front of all the other kids, made a public speech identifying me and Riccardo saying that what we were doing was a disgraceful sin and should not happen again.

Still in my last year at the institute I remember a girl come to stay with us. I never seen a girl there before and I don't know why she was there. She was younger and she would sleep apart from the boys in the assistants' room and during the day was never left on her own.

Although he looked dangerous – tattoos, gold teeth, piercings and shaved bald – he smiled a lot, was passionate about making 'work'... and danced beautifully.

David Clark Allen, artist

The photographs will show the mess and the pain. They will have some of the beauty and terror perhaps the spill and swing of a Franko B performance. But always, somewhere near the end when Franko looks into the darkness and the audience looks back and eye meets eye there is not an image to take because this is an exchange, of another light, that is only human.

Hugo Glendinning, photographer

Another time I remember how one of us was in the infirmary where sometimes when we were sick we would end up staying. Next to it there was the director's office and on the other side her living quarters with her private toilet and bathroom that the sick kids staying in the infirmary had to use. We also used her bottles of perfumes and once the director noticed she went insane!

During our walks out and about in Mergozzo, especially when I reached the age of 13 and over, I was more aware of what was happening around me and I realised how the people and the boys of the town of Mergozzo looked at us, the boys of the Red Cross, in a weird way, sometimes with an undisguised superiority. My feelings were shifting from sickness to shame.

Once in a while we would walk alongside a huge mansion where often there was a child that seemed very happy playing on his bike or with his parents. I would look at him, and wished that I had a life like him. Why I dint have a normal family as he had? But of course I dint have an idea what life this child was having, it could actually have been worse than mine.

By spring 1974 the institute had about 80 boys raging from 7 years old to 15 years old maximum. I think that 65% of the boys were under 12 years old. The other 35%, which I was part of, was from 12 years old to 15 years old. So the ones that had reached the teen years like me were moved to another building and were in social groups where our ages were very similar.

The building where the bigger boys slept and socialised out of the class was in a new, purpose built 2-storey building, we called it the 'Casa Blanca' (the white house) because it was a large white house and was about 30 yards away at the back of the main building where the other 65% lived and went to school. We in year 5 even had another smaller building next to the white house where we spent our time when not in class, and the small football pitch and table games were based there for us.

Also in the last year the assistants that were looking after us in normal daytime were not sleeping in the same building as us when they were on night duty with the smaller kids. Instead at the white house I remember we had one of the nuns living on the ground floor to keep an ear and eye on us above her. And she bloody did.

In the white house dormitory everything was possible: solitary, mutual and group masturbation, and of course blow jobs. In the last few months before my leaving the Red Cross Institute I was regularly masturbating with other boys from one-to-one to groups of 4-5 in the toilet next to our dormitory, in the afternoon after school and before we went to bed and sometimes in the middle of the night with one boy in particular, Fernando.

He was probably the oldest boy and one of the boys I was masturbating in the group with usually. He liked getting sucked off by boys a year or so younger or smaller than him (yes, the same Fernando from the Biandrate days that 5 years or so previously had bullied me into giving him all Mother's money from the kitchen window).

Fernando was aggressive like his brothers... especially as he was older and full of testosterone. He was the classic alpha man. He coincidently arrived at the Red Cross Institute about 2 years after I arrived there. I assume that the local primary school in Biandrate must have refused to have him or was beyond 'normal' education and for sure, based what I knew about him he needed some kind of help and discipline and very likely dint regularly attend school. Our social backgrounds were very similar, although with different personal circumstances.

I think that nobody in my age group that I was in class or after class grouping with was gay or homosexual, not consciously, although nobody knew what being gay meant or was. There was not any sexual education at all. It was taboo to just have the physical urge to masturbate and getting pleasure from it was a taboo also. And of course there was a competitiveness to it: who come more or who could come more times? Who was harder? Who had a bigger cock? Etc... etc...

I have to say there never was tenderness or intimacy as such, it was more mechanical – an urge and something to do, something that happened naturally if you were a boy going through puberty age, which we were. If you shared a room with other boys of your age between 10 and 15 years old you cannot hide these urges for long.

I remember that we were not supposed to sleep naked but of course once the assistant or the nuns went to their own room, we would. Our room probably smelt so much of testosterone and cum that one could get high on it. Anyway the priest and Luigi seemed very keen to find out what we were up to, especially with the older boys like me and Fernando and the ones in my year in the last 2 years at the Red Cross.

I remember my teacher Luigi, one morning in our class he started looking at us in the eyes and saying that he could tell from our faces that we were touching ourselves and the priest also, some time before Luigi did, said the same thing to me. I was alone with him in the chapel and he asked me 'do you touch yourself?' At first I was confused but after he asked me more times I got what he meant and of course I said 'no, I don't touch myself'.

Sex apart, those who were sleeping in our dormitory at the white house sometimes would sneak out for night trips. We would go down to the lake or up to the wood just next the institute (a tiny place called Bracchio). We would hide ourselves when a car was passing and after few hours we would go back to the dormitory. Two boys once ran away and never come back.

About a month before leaving the institute, while hanging in the living room in the main building where the younger kids were living, I popped in to Beata (one of the sadistic assistants) and in that very moment she was beating a very small child. I don't know why but my instinct made me go up to her and told her to stop it. She turned to me and she was going to slap me, but I jumped on a stool that was nearby and got to the same height as her and I slapped her instead.

She was shocked and could not respond. Of course this was not going to be the end of it.

The following day I was called to the director's office in front of the director of the institute with Beata present. They were waiting for me. Beata had already told her side of the story. It was not a pleasant moment as both shouted at me then Beata ordered me to hold my hands down close to my body and proceeded to give me the hardest single slap she could have given to me. After that I was forced to unconditionally apologise to her and the director for what I did.

The first thing I thought of was that authority was disgusting and gives some people the right to abuse it and abuse others. It was in that moment I realised how this would have been at the root of my making. I felt powerless and it made me dislike bullies and all institutions that could have control over your life while abusing anyone and getting away with it.

Around May, or June '74, when I was 14, I sadly realised that my time at the Red Cross was at an end. I had just finished primary school and I was too anti- authority and a troubled teen and after my incident with Beata, which I thought was self-defence against a bully, the institute decided that I was too much of a risk. It was going to be too much trouble to try to find me another place where I could have carried on with my secondary education away from my family.

I think they could not really be bothered to care for me – I was not their responsibility anymore. I had a family somewhere, a fucked up one but still my legal guardians, so they decided to wash their hands so to speak. I dint deserve their protection any longer. My rebellion or my fuck you anti-authority stance dint do me any favours (at least it looked that way, but now I actually think it saved me).

So it was back to my blood family residence at Cascina La Ca Peregallo / Lesmo in province of Milan.

Some time at the end of June in that hot summer, I was dispatched back with my mother. I believe a social worker brought me back home to them. This was the second and final time since the Easter break few months before.

Soon I found out that my mother was more or less the same desperate mental self as I experienced her the first time I met her years earlier. I realised that she dint have any intention to send me to secondary school. She wanted me to get a job in order for me to help the family. I was 14 and half years old.

One of the features of the new house where we were now living was that the toilet was at about 50 yards outside the actual house at the back of the house through a shared courtyard, and soon I become the bucket's attendant boy. Which meant that every single night I had to take this bucket full of shit and piss, which belonged to my family, to the outside toilet to dispose its lovely contents while trying to hold my breath. I remember I would wait till it was very late at night to carry out this task because I was so embarrassed in case I bumped to people in the street while I was taking it – it would have been obvious what my cargo was.

Straight after me coming back to the family I had a huge argument with my mother as I wanted to go back to school. She replied that the family did not have money, thus I had to go to work and help the family – it was my duty (by the way she was not working). It was up to my stepfather to find me a job and soon he did. This was as an apprentice in a car crash repair garage not far from our house. I think that I worked there for a few months, maybe 3 to 5 months or so. At the beginning I remember I found it very hard.

My first work boss was Mario, originally from the south Italian region of Calabria. He had 2 big guard dogs, German Shepherds, and I had to clean up their shit every morning. What I remember of Mario was that he was the typical heterosexual chauvinistic male one encountered in those times. He owned sport cars and seemed very popular with 'the ladies'. Once he kicked me very hard for something I was supposed to have done wrong or that he dint like and I remember he made me cry. After this he seemed nicer to me.

While I was working for Mario I found another part-time job. During the weekends I was washing dishes in a pizzeria that belonged to one of Mario's customers, which was how we met. He was from Milan and his name was Franco and I remember that also he once kicked me for being slow at washing up, so I ran home and few hours later he came to my house to ask me to go back. I did go back for a while as I dint have a choice.

Eventually, after years, my stepfather's relatives found out officially of my existence; I then met his mother and sisters. My stepfather's mother was old but cool and I would go to visit her with the twins quite often as she wasn't living more than 200 yards from our home.

Once, me and the family went to a wedding of one of my cousins from my mother's side. He was an ex-aspirant boxer in his teens living in Gardone Val Trompia (which is where my mother originally come from) and once there I had the chance to meet all my relatives from my mother's side for the first time ever.

We went there for a few days before the wedding, even though I dint want to go – I wished to go and visit Raffaella, the ex-assistant at the Red Cross Institute. For that wish I still have a small scar, on the right side of my head, just above my eye between the temple and the eye, that my mother provided me with using an old piece of iron from our stove in the house. We had a disagreement about going to the wedding and my mother beat me up and won. So I had to go.

It was during those days in Gardone Val Trompia that I experienced personally for the first time racist abuse towards me. It made me think that perhaps my real father probably was from the south of Italy as few people would shout at me the sort of abuse that racist northerners would shout at a southerner. Maybe it was just the way I looked.

Once at home, I remember I tried to make a contact with my ex-teacher Luigi by writing him a letter. In that period I was so desperate, isolated and lonely, I was missing the institute and the friends I had there. I wasn't happy at all back home with my mother and stepfather.

Luigi did reply to my lonely and probably desperate letter, but I seem to remember that its response was not nice somehow. He wrote me that he had a little girl and because of that, he dint want me to visit him because he wouldn't want his daughter to come into contact with someone like me, or something like this...

Back home I remember I met one of my stepfather's sisters called Antonia, she owned a hairdressing salon. She was another class apart from my stepfather and us because she married well with a local doctor. I think she felt genuinely sorry for me and thought that I could do a better job than working at car repairs for Mario and at Franco's pizzeria.

One day, it must have been 1975 by now and I must have been back home with my family about 7 months or so... I was 15 and I remember it was raining a lot outside and I was working at the pizzeria washing up and cleaning in the kitchen. The restaurant was empty and my stepfather's sister Antonia came to the pizzeria and told me to drop everything and go with her because she got me a better job. She must have known that Franco was not a nice person.

She found me a job as apprentice in a small metalwork factory that was making components for car batteries. I think that the owner's name was Pier Luigi. The factory was in the town of Lesmo, about 4 kilometres from my house. I was the youngest apprentice in this small family-run business.

I would go to work by bicycle, riding on a very steep hill which meant that coming back down was usually fun and sometimes dangerous. I would work 5 days and a half every week. I don't remember what I was getting paid but I was 'legal' for the first time and treated fairly and the owners never kicked me if I made an error.

I had to give my pay to my mother and in turn she would give me 150 lire per week, for personal use which meant hardly anything. It was enough to buy a ticket to see a film on a Sunday afternoon at the local cinema, with of course the presence of my 3 smaller sisters. This was because when I was not at work to earn money I was at the service of my mother's needs and wishes, especially looking after my sisters when they were not at school, sometimes cooking for them if my mother dint want to, going to the next town to do the shopping or looking for my stepfather to ask him for money. I hardly was permitted to have time for myself or freedom to go out on my own. I had to fight for it or find schemes to do it or take advantage of my mother's good moods when they happened.

Usually I had to have my 3 sisters in tow if I went out of the house for anything that was not work or my mother's needs because my mother dint trust me to be alone outside. My sisters were her eyes and ears and a deterrent to stop me doing things that would have got me in trouble back at home. But fortunately in that period I become friendly with a girl and a boy just a few yards from my house.

The girl was in her late teens and was living in a flat exactly facing mine across the street. I could talk to her from my mother's bedroom upstairs. Her family was very poor, like mine, or perhaps even more so. The difference was that their toilet was inside her flat but right next to their cooking stove in their kitchen. She had lots of sisters and brothers and they were from Napoli. They did remind me a bit of Fernando and his family back in Biandrate, but they were nicer people.

Through the girl from Napoli, I met her boyfriend. His name was Andrea and he was a young cook from the region of Val D'Aosta, on the border with France on the Alps side. He was working as a cook in a restaurant in the next town and had a room in a house in the same courtyard as I was living. He was in his early 20s I think. It is unfortunate that I don't remember exactly his full name as later on he was instrumental (although I think not consciously) in helping me to get away from my family.

In the same building, downstairs, there was my only male friend. He was Enrico who lived alone with his father who was a long distance lorry driver. Enrico was a year younger or so than me and also dint go to school anymore, so he was at home alone most of the time. When I could I would sneak out of my house and go across the road to see them without my sisters in tow. Then eventually I would hear my mother screaming from our window: 'Franco disgraziato ma che fai? Vieni a casa ad aiutarmi!' – *Franco you are a disgrace! Come home now to help me!!*

Once, Enrico and I went to a swimming pool in the town of Arcore. It was an outdoor swimming pool so it reminded me of my time at the Red Cross, but it was much much larger. I looked at the other boys jumping into the water and they looked so happy so I decided to jump in myself. I soon realised the difference between the Red Cross swimming pool and this one. This was deeper and I could not swim but somehow I forgot this detail. I remember that I panicked but the lifeguard was near and grabbed me and pulled me out of the pool. I was so embarrassed.

--–

As I said before, when I was not at work I would be doing things for my mother and I remember on one occasion I was sent to Arcore to do some shopping. She gave me 10,000 lire and a list of what I had to buy for the week. Most of the money was spent on some red meat at the butcher's shop (red meat was a rare thing in our house because we were very poor but usually indulged in it at the end of the month or when I or my stepfather got paid from work.)

On my way back from this shopping trip I had to stop at the chemist, so I parked the bike on the side of the road with the shopping bags from the butcher on it, but when I came out of the chemist and got my bike to my shock and surprise I noticed that the shopping wasn't there anymore. Someone had stolen it.

I knew that mother would get mad – very mad – and in fact she did. She started screaming, pulling her hair, throwing herself on the floor, throwing things at me that she could immediately get hold of and accusing me of having spent the money on something for me, which there was no evidence of.

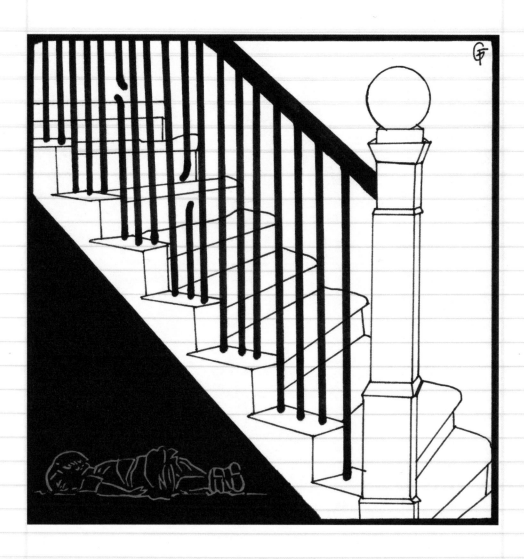

At a certain point I was so scared that I ran away and slept for 1 whole night in the under the stairs outside Enrico's house. I remember that it was a cold and wet night.

The next day a truce was eventually organised between me and my mother with the help of some of the neighbours that got involved. When it was fairly safe to go back in the house, my mother brought me to the butcher shop in Arcore to ask if I did buy the meat 2 days earlier, which the butcher confirmed and ensured her that I actually bought the meat with the money, although he dint know what I did with it once I left the shop.

My stepfather dint spend much time at home. He said that he was working all the time, night and day. He was back home once or twice a week and usually when he was depressed and crazy. He would come home and my mother would give him a hard time about money, where he had been etc... etc...

Sometimes this was not good for all of us in the house, including my mother, because he would freak out and get in a very deep depression, which meant usually spending 2-3 days in bed and throwing shoes or anything reachable from the bed at anyone that bothered him or was simply trying to get him to get up and go to work or to give us some money.

Me and my sisters were living in terror when he was at home. Any of us could have got a beating during the night when we were asleep. Going to bed was dangerous; so many times we would just sleep downstairs in the one kitchen and living room area on chairs or the one sofa we had.

For our immediate next door neighbours and those in our courtyard this very public evil in our house was kind of a routine and not so amusing anymore, although sometimes some of the neighbours would try to intervene, especially when it would spill into the courtyard because I ran out of the house to escape the furore or the imminent danger posed by my mother or stepfather. Usually it was my mother that would start throwing things out of the window of the main bedroom on the first floor of our house. Usually these things happened to be my belongings, like once my record player or books or presents that people had given me, my clothes or whatever she could get her hands on that had to do with me.

In the summer of 1975, just a year since I had come back home from the Red Cross Institute for good, I had had enough of my family and I swallowed all the pills that I found in the house but my mother realised what I did as stupidly I had left a suicide note (hahahhahahha).

As it happened my stepfather was at home or just come back in that moment and woke me up by slapping me and making me vomit. I felt very sick for a few days but I dint die.

A few days later I decided to go to the police station (the Carabinieri) in the town of Arcore to report the abuse I was getting from my parents, hoping that they would call some kind of social services or minors' protection agency and put me in some institute to protect me from my family.

Once at the police station I explained what was happening and that I needed help so they took me in a room where there was a police officer sergeant type and he asked me why I was there in the first place. So I told him that I wanted to report my mother and stepfather for abusing me and that I needed protection and that I dint want to live with them anymore and that I was 15 years old and a minor.

He looked at me, and when I finished he said to me, while he was taking off his belt, that I was lucky enough to not be his own son, otherwise he would have beaten me himself. He then told me to go back home, which I did.

A while later I found out that the sergeant at the police station of Arcore where I went to report my family for abusing me knew my stepfather and his family very well, and that they often played cards together at the bar in town. As a result my secret was out. He told my stepfather what I had done and it was not pleasant.

Sometimes, while outside because I had been threatened by my mother or stepfather, I was able to go back home thanks to some of the neighbours who would get involved to try to calm the situation.

In times of peace, if my stepfather was not to be seen for few days (my mother used to accuse him of seeing another woman in Arcore) my mother would send me look for him, usually in bars or at one of his jobs. Apart from a night shift in a factory as a security guard (apparently), he was working in

63

a petrol station owned by Agip as a forecourt attendant, serving motorists.

Most of the time, the moment he would see me he would gesticulate for me to go away and eventually to fuck off but this was not an option for me as my failure to get anything that was remotely positive out of him would have made my mother pissed off with me instead. It was always a no-win situation. So it meant 'don't go home till you get something from the bastard' and I would stand on the side of the road and wait, sometimes for hours.

Eventually he would give in and give me some money to take home, or get some food to take home. I remember one day, a customer, while I was waiting in the petrol station, asked my stepfather who I was, or if I was his son? To which my stepfather replied NO! ... I was just the bastard son of his wife.

Another question that used to be asked was 'What did my mother do in the daytime? Did she work?' My mother was classified as a housewife; she cooked sometimes and made beds sometimes (I made my own). Usually I had to help her with cleaning and washing up and I did all the shopping.

She tended to go out to visit a couple of people she got on with in the community. One was Rosina or Rosa, a very old lady that was living all alone for many years (her husband died a long time before) and another woman that was married and had a small son (I don't remember their names). They lived near us and they tended to be in their houses most days.

I remember my mother liked to buy or swap journals / magazines, like romantic stories illustrated by photographs with captions (*photos romanzi storie*) and sometimes pornos that I would find under mattresses. She looked at them when my stepfather was not around and she would hide them when he was because he would accuse her of wasting his money.

One day I left the job at the metal industry factory that my step auntie Antonia got me. I don't know why or how long I was there for but it could not have been much longer than 6 months, although it seemed years. So my stepfather found me a job as plumber's apprentice with someone he knew from Arcore.

I had 2 bosses: one played the good cop so to speak and the other, the bad cop. I dint last long, maybe a month or so.

One day we were a bit far away from where I was living – maybe 20 / 30 kilometres or so – installing the plumbing on a new building development. In the middle of the afternoon the bad cop one was being verbally nasty and playing mind games with me, so I decided there and then that I had had enough. I just walked out on him without saying anything – I just walked away, got onto the road and started to hitchhike.

Eventually a car stopped and I went back home. Later on that night he come to the house, asking me if I was intending to go back to work the following day. I said no even though I knew my mother and stepfather would not have been happy about it. In fact the next day I was back at work with them, but this time with the good cop.

I worked for them till before Christmas 1975. By this time I had been at home with my blood family for about 18 months and it seemed an eternity.

A day before New Year Eve of 1975, the boyfriend of my Naples friend asked me if I wanted to work for New Year's Eve in a town a bit far away at Villa d'Adda Alta near the city of Bergamo. The owners of a restaurant / pizzeria were looking for someone to do the dishwashing. As I wasn't working in that period I accepted the offer and I went.

I think it was about 1 hour or so from my family house but it was far if you dint have a car. I spent 2 days away and I liked it and the owner liked me and before I left on the 2nd of January 1976 he asked me if I wanted the job permanently, as a wash up and general kitchen cleaner. He would give me boarding / accommodation and food on top of my wage.

I could not believe what an opportunity it was – to leave home – and I said yes. Now I had to convince my mother that it was a good idea, also for her, but I knew it would be difficult.

Of course she got angry at me and said 'NO!' Her argument was... 'I need you here to help with the house and to look after your sisters...' I begged her, saying I would come back once a week and, with the promise to give her my entire wage every month, I asked her to let me try it for a month at least.

She insisted that it was not going to happen, but I insisted that it was going to happen, even if she dint like it. She got mad and tried to beat me up but this time I stood firm and, in self-defence, slapped her back. She tried to hit me, then threw a ceramic vase that was on the table at me. I managed to duck and it missed me, so she tried to hit me with a wooden stick and pull my hair and called me a disgrace but I grabbed the stick away from her and pushed her away. I told her that it was over and that I would not take her shit and I realised for the first time that I was much stronger than her, physically and also mentally. She also realised for the first time that it was over, her grip on me was gone and that she had lost control over me for good. So she warned me of the consequences when my stepfather come back home... that he is going to sort me out and that I will pay for it... I say ok.

In the mean time I decided to go upstairs to my room and get some of my clothes together to take with me to my new destination as I was not going to spend another night in my family house. I knew that it was not safe place to be once my stepfather got home. When he eventually did get back that same evening, my mother told him what was happening and he told me to do what my mother says, or else...

I tell them that I am leaving home and, if they don't like it, to call the police. They tell me that I'm a minor and I have to do what they say. Then my stepfather tries to grab me but I'm on alert and I go for the door so he grabs a large kitchen knife and chases me into the street. It is a cold and wet January night. He is wearing only his pants, a camisole and slippers.

I run for my life for about 30 yards with him running after me with the knife. Meanwhile my mother is throwing things out of the first floor window of our house into the street and shouting something at me. I can't remember exactly what happened just after this but lucky for me, my stepfather ran out of steam and I got away from him.

I made my way to the town of Arcore with a bag with few clothes that I managed to collect from what my mother chucked out of the window.

Eventually I met up with Andrea (the cook) who come to pick me up in a car that another guy called Mario was driving (he was a waiter from Avellino that was going to work and live in the same restaurant complex as me) and we left the town of Arcore for good.

It was the 3rd or 4th of January 1976, 3 weeks short of my 16th birthday, and escaping my blood family was the best birthday present I ever got or could ever have given to myself.

So now I was in Villa d'Adda Alta, working for Aldo in his restaurant and sharing a room with the cook and the waiter (Andrea and Mario). The restaurant / pizzeria wasn't going so well customers-wise, while the discotheque below was very busy at the weekend with young people (but older than me).

The discotheque was owned and run by somebody else but on a Sunday afternoon I would be allowed in and I loved it. It played a mix of dance / disco music, pop and rock, from Donna Summer to Queen. I become friendly with the DJ and his best mate; they were about 4-5 years older than me and about to be called for national military service. I liked them.

My relationship with Andrea and Mario was kind of strange... They treated me a bit like a boy where they were men, especially Mario, who was I think in his mid-late 20s. I was too young to hang around with them.

Mario was a typical Italian man of that period – macho, hetero, homophobic, stupid, cocky. Andrea seemed bullied by Mario. He once said that he would beat me up if he discovered that I was gay. (To be honest I was not yet fully conscious of what that meant, although I never had a romantic or sexual encounter with a girl and when I masturbated and stuck objects like pens up my bum I was thinking of boys.)

As I said, I was sharing a big room with Andrea and Mario. The room had 3 or 4 beds and there were the 3 of us who worked and lived together, but not really together as such – we were together because of circumstance. They were migrant workers from other parts of Italy and me, I dint know what I was, I was maybe just on the run from my family, except they were not looking for me or reported me to the police because I was a minor. Back then one was a minor till the age of 21, and I was 16 and looked out of place most of the time.

I think we had 1 day off a week, on a Tuesday. Most of the time I spent it on my own except once with Mario and Andrea in Mario's car. We passed a prostitute on the road and Mario said that he would pay for me to have sex with her so I would prove that I was not gay and that I liked women.

She was on the side of the street on a country road with a metal bucket that had a fire in it, I suppose to keep her warm and to be more visible. I agreed, I suppose, to prove to Mario and Andrea that I was not gay, but Mario had said that he would beat me up if I was. So Mario arranged with the prostitute to have sex in the car with all 3 of us, one by one, for an agreed price.

Mario adjusted the front seats so we could lay down with more comfort I suppose, and he decided that I should go first.

Me and the woman got in the car. I remember she looked at me and said, 'you never done this before have you?' and I said 'no, it's my first time' so she put a condom on my penis while explaining what it was for.

The problem is that I'm not turned on and it's difficult to put the condom on a limp penis. She started saying that I needed to get it up and that I'm running out of time with her for the fee Mario has paid. A few times she tries to get me to lay on top of her but it's not working and I can see Mario and Andrea looking in the direction of the car to see if there is movement, which is not helping either.

Soon she said 'look, it's ok if you don't like girls but I cannot waste time here with you, I will tell your friends that you did good with me'. So I said 'ok please do, otherwise they will beat me up' (at least I believed this). I got out of the car and the two 'real' men were looking at me and then at her and then she said 'come on, quick, who's next?'

After about 15 minutes we were all 'done' with her and we left her at the side of the street to go back to the restaurant / home. In the car they asked me how it was... I say that it was very good and Mario confirms that the prostitute had said that I did good so everybody is happy.

After a month or so at the restaurant at Villa D'Adda, a meeting was called by Aldo, the owner, and his accountant. They told us that the business was doing very badly and that they need to close the restaurant immediately but they have another 2 restaurants / pizzerias a hour away by car, at Fino Mornasco near the city of Como on the Italian Swiss border and Cantù. He says I can go to live and work there if I wanted. Of course I wanted. I was on my own and I would have been homeless if I dint.

The other restaurants were run by family, and were about 5 kilometres apart from each other. One was run by Aldo's mum and the other by his dad (this was because they were actually separated).

At first I worked and lived at Aldo's mum's pizzeria. The pizzeria was very busy, especially on a Sunday evening. I was working very hard at making sure we dint run out of clean plates and cutlery. Aldo's mother was in her 60s and very demanding and I could see why nobody in her family wanted to work in her restaurant.

I think I was with her for about a month and then I got transferred to the other restaurant's pizzeria where the rest of Aldo's family worked. It was situated in a *cascina* (farmhouse) that was called La Costa and the pizzeria had the same name if I remember right. It was situated on top of a small hill, about 3 kilometres from Como.

The cook of the restaurant was Aldo's wife. Her name was Donatella and Aldo's brother, Angelo, was the *pizzaiolo* / pizza-man. He was a hippy and smoked lots of dope, and sometimes Donatella and Aldo's father and Angelo would smoke too.

I had the impression that Aldo's brother and father dint really like me but nevertheless quickly I became part of the family thanks to Donatella and Aldo. It was Donatella being an outsider herself in that situation that meant she took me under her protective wing and made sure I was not exploited or abused in any way.

Her situation was also strange. Aldo was a bit of a playboy, especially when he often travelled to 'exotic places' like South America for a few months at time, although he had a very young daughter with Donatella, called Nina if I remember right. Their relationship was kept together by the fact they were legally married and had a kid, which was typical of many families in Italy in the 1970s. I think that perhaps they were separated but not officially – let's say that a working-class woman with a young child leaving her husband was not a practical thing to do back then.

Most days I would start work at 10am and work till 3pm then restart at 5.30pm and work to 12.30am, 6 days a week for almost 2 and a half years.

Me and Angelo were living above the restaurant but had our own room. For the first year or so we dint have a shower or a bath in the building, just a sink and a toilet in the courtyard. The building was very old and cold. Eventually Aldo's father agreed to get a shower installed and I remember it was pure luxury for me.

I seem to remember the restaurant was closed on a Tuesday so it was my day off but, especially early on when I just moved there when I dint know anyone, I was frequently alone and Donatella would take me with her and her family. They used to do excursions and try other restaurants in other places, sometimes we would travel hours to do this. There was nothing else to do I suppose.

One day as I was working on my evening shift, the restaurant was busy and I was busy washing up, my mother pulled up in a car at the back where the kitchen was. I don't remember how she found me but she did. This was the first time I had seen her in more than a year.

She was accompanied by a shopkeeper who stated that I had left a huge debt while he was giving me goods, on credit, for me and my family when I was 15 years old and so now he wanted the money back. I reminded him that he knew that it was my mother that was responsible for the debt as the shopping was for my family. Donatella dint let them finish and told them to be ashamed and basically to get off her property and not to dare to ever come back, telling them to never come back or else.

Strangely, the man was a relative of my stepfather and would have been fully aware of the situation from the start. Probably when he confronted my mother about it she must have had the grand idea to try to bully me into paying for it. My mother must have thought that I was still very much her property legally as I was a minor.

Donatella encouraged me to try to get better education for myself. She told me that if I wanted I could go to a special school in Como, the Institute Minerva. It was an adult education place where I could do my secondary education and there was a 1 year course that would have allowed me to do the 3 years of *scuole medie* / secondary school in one academic year. It was a private school basically, but I could afford it because I was working. (Because I was young, I would ask for money when I needed it rather than cashing my wage at the end of the month. When I needed extra money sometimes in the week, Donatella would give it to me from my wage. When eventually I left this job in January 1979, at the age of 19, I had what was for me at that time good savings from the accumulated wages over the 2 and half or so years I was there.)

So I decided to try the private school with Donatella's moral support. She allowed me to leave work at lunchtime 1 hour before usual and start work in the evening 1 hour later, 3 days a week. So I started to go to Como to study, but also I started to make some friends. Aldo's family were not happy at first, they always felt that Donatella favoured me too much.

After few months working in Donatella's restaurant, helping her with the dishes, I soon become her assistant. I was frying chips and some fish for her in the deep fryer, and doing vegetable and general prep for her and for Angelo and his pizza making, doing the sides and preparing the ingredients for pizzas. Donatella decided then to employ another guy who could do the dishwashing, so after a while a new guy come. His name was also Mario, maybe a year older than me, and we become very close friends.

At the same time my social life become busier and busier, even though it was now concentrated in the public square of Como. Most of the people I knew were older than me and with varied experiences with politics and drugs. These were the main issues discussed amongst us.

I remember after reading an article about the Sex Pistols (I can't remember where, possibly at a friend's place in Como), I realised that I was a punk. I read about England and I was fascinated by it; from this abstract distance people seemed to have more fun and to be more free. They dint have the pope, being a homosexual was not a crime any longer, boys could be girls and vice versa. I dint know what I was in term of sexually but I knew that I liked boys and that I felt more intimate with them than girls, but I was never able to talk about it openly with people I knew or considered friends, maybe because these friendships never lasted for a very long time.

I loved Patti Smith, Lou Reed, David Bowie, Jack Kerouac, William Burroughs, Pink Floyd. I recall I would wear welding goggles and bleach / peroxide my hair, with bleached tight trousers and yellow plastic boots with my ears pierced, which at that time was not considered right for a man to have. It challenged the concept of masculinity. Some hippies had it but only in one ear.

In the Como public square, those who belonged politically to the left were on one side of the main square keeping themselves separate from those from the right that were on the other side of the square. Whenever I was going through the square it was possible that I would get bothered by both groups; the ones from the left would call me fascist and the ones on the right, a freak or *froscio*, Italian slang for homosexual. I had to be careful around both groups, punk was not big in Como or Italy for what I knew, certainly I was the only punk in Como when I lived there.

At the Institute Minerva I made friends with a boy who was catching up with his study like me. He identified himself with the MSI, the Italian fascist movement, but was totally cool with me, and one day when a group of his friends tried to beat me up he intervened and stopped it. He told me that he was a fascist to piss his parents off as they were prominent local communist politicians.

I also had friends on the left, some members of more radical groups like Lotta Continua, a far-left extra-parliamentary organisation. Others were just drug users and funnily enough they dint care about me.

When I was not at school or work at the pizzeria I was around Como square or with my friend Mario from the kitchen. Mario was from Cantù and was from a large family, his father had died some time when he was small. After work me and Mario would go to my room and drink wine, or take LSD. Once we decided to try heroin. It was not nice and we both ended up vomiting.

I also owned a Vespa scooter and once I remember I was so high that I had an accident by driving the wrong way on the road. But I was lucky, I just dislocated a shoulder.

Around the farmhouse there were another 2 or 3 families that were very much related to each other. They had some animals. They all looked inbred. There was a man and a young woman: he was her uncle and she looked more like a man that he did. One day they both started working in the pizzeria as waiters. She was called Orietta (eventually she started to go out with Angelo the pizza-man) and it was obvious her uncle was homosexual but it was never talked about openly.

He was in his mid-30s and not married, still living with his whole family. Sometimes I would go to his house and one day without saying anything he gave me a plastic bag with a bunch of gay porn magazines, which I was very happy to have. I think that we both knew of each other's sexuality but we never actually said anything about it.

After my 18th birthday in 1978 I had to go to the city of Monza as I had received a letter from the military service back home. My mother must have forwarded it on to me as she knew where I was living. So I went to Como main train station to look at train times, probably to go the next day.

While I was looking at the timetable noticeboard this man approached me and asked me if I wanted to have a glass of wine or two... I said 'why not?' although once outside the station he asked me if I was aware of what he really wanted from me. I said that I knew what he wanted and I was cool about it. So I followed him, he must have been in his 40s or so.

He took me to a seedy hotel near the station and I had my first anal intercourse. He asked me if I had had sex with men before. I told him that I did have some masturbatory sex with boys and men before but that I was a virgin. He was a good fuck, it hurt but I loved it, but he dint believe me that I never got fucked before, even though there was blood from my ass all over his dick and the bed sheets. Anyway the morning after I left the hotel while he was still asleep and I have never ever seen him again.

After the first medical check at the Monza military base, the military reported me to a military clinic / hospital in Milano to have a further visit and interview with army medical staff. I assume this was because I looked very different from your normal 18 year old boy / man.

Every time we went over as a family, everywhere you
looked, the rooms were black. Hidden within was a glossy,
explicit pinball machine, reaching far above my young
hands. I coveted that the most as a child.

Seth Randall, friend

Umanità è la parola che erige come porta bandiera, occupa
tutta la sua persona e ha occupato me.

Humanity is the word that stands as a flag carrier,
occupies all of his person and occupied me.

Nicholas Polari, student

Every time I see a video Franko gave me in the 1990s of a
performance where he is standing, naked, alone and completely
painted white while bleeding in front of the audience, it
gives me back the image of a guy with a huge heart, a great
artist and someone very special. I'm lucky enough to have
matched this life with Franko B. Franko, I love you.

Marcel.li Antúnez Roca, artist

Their first diagnosis was that I had schizophrenic and neurotic tendencies. Despite this issue the military doctors decided that I was suitable for military service. I personally tried to avoid doing the compulsory service by stating that I took drugs but the doctor colonel responded to me saying that he was doing more drugs than me.

In the same year, in September 1978, I decided to go on holiday on my own for the first time. I took a month off from work at the pizzeria at the farmhouse, and planned to reach my destination of Sardinia by hitchhiking till Civitavecchia, the old city from the Roman times, where I would get a boat to the island.

I dint really know why I wanted to go there, except that my friend Riccardo from my time at the Red Cross was from Cagliari in Sardinia, or maybe someone might have suggested it to me.

During this travelling adventure through central Italy I would get many lifts to the next place on the way towards my destination, sometimes with no logical route, and exclusively from men drivers. By now I was well aware of the high possibility of having some kind of sex with some of them, and I was actually looking forward to it.

Usually it would start like this: 'How old are you? Got a girlfriend? Where are your parents?' Then at the first opportunity they would get off the main road or motorway and take their cocks out and I would oblige. Sometimes they would buy me some food to eat, sometimes not. Sometimes I would ask for cash to buy cigarettes.

One of my stops was in Genoa, with one of mother's brothers that I never met before. I don't remember his name. He had a girl and a boy. The boy was 15 and on the first night, weirdly my auntie made me sleep in his bed with him.

Yes I was his cousin but I was 18 years old and never met him before. To me he was a stranger and I did want to have sex with him. He was cute, but I dint. Though the day afterwards my uncle and aunt must have realised the situation could have been awkward as they moved me to another room in the house that was probably a store / spare room.

I stayed there 8 or 10 days and a few times I went to work with my uncle. He was in the removal business, driving a removal / delivery truck. I really liked this time with him and also I got on well with my cousin, he was sweet.

Once I left Genoa I went to Orvieto to pay a visit to Donatella's older sister who I had met many times at the pizzeria as she used to come to visit frequently with her son and her husband. I stayed with them for 1 night before I travelled to Civitavecchia where I took the ferry to Porto del Golfo Aranci / Sardinia. On the boat I met a couple of guys who I would spend the following two weeks with while in Sardinia. One was from Pordenone, the other from Udine.

My hair was orange from strong bleaching and after about one week in the sun I was dark brown with orange hair.

After my month off work I went back to the pizzeria. I was changed, I felt I wanted to travel more, and also decided not to take my secondary school final exam. I could not care for it any more so I dint get the qualification. Instead, I still just had my primary school qualification from the Red Cross Institute. I remember that Donatella and my Italian class teacher were not very happy with my decision, but it was my life after all.

I remained at the pizzeria working with Donatella and the family for 4 months, till just after my 19th birthday. I had accumulated a little fortune from my wages, and I asked Donatella to keep some money for me for later on when I eventually came back. Everybody at the pizzeria and farmhouse thought that I would come back and ask for my job back. Also Donatella told me that there was always a place to work and live with her at the pizzeria if I ever did want to come back.

My idea was to go and pay a visit to one of the guys I had met on the ferry to Sardinia a few months earlier. He had given me his address and told me to visit him. His family owned a bar near Pordenone and the first night they made me sleep in a type of farmhouse outside town. I remember it was terribly cold, so the following night, they had me stay in a flat they owned in town. I can't remember how long I stayed there. I guess less than a week. They were hospitable but it was very cold and the town looked miserable in the winter. There was nothing to do there and so I would go for walks in the afternoons.

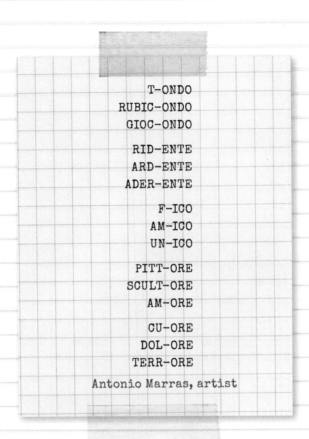

```
            T-ONDO
        RUBIC-ONDO
         GIOC-ONDO

          RID-ENTE
          ARD-ENTE
        ADER-ENTE

            F-ICO
           AM-ICO
           UN-ICO

         PITT-ORE
        SCULT-ORE
           AM-ORE

           CU-ORE
          DOL-ORE
         TERR-ORE
```

Antonio Marras, artist

When I was three we had a brilliant day in the park on
the swings but then his dog ate my favourite football.
I think I cried.

Zeb Randall, friend

While walking I one day I noticed there was a funeral. I don't know why but I started to follow the cortège to the cemetery. From a certain distance I would look at the people crying, others moved, and I suddenly recall another funeral I had seen at my mother's village a few years before. It was the funeral of a young boy from south Italy who had been killed by a car. I remember how the relatives were crying loud, all the shouting and the theatrical drama. This funeral I was witnessing in this town was instead calm and silent.

I started to be moved by it too and I started crying, but I dint know why. I was not attached to this person or place or people. Then I realised that people were looking at me, asking themselves perhaps who the fuck I was. So silently I left.

Next stop: Udine, to visit the other guy from the Sardinia ferry. The day I arrived (unannounced) he was about to leave for his university in Trieste, so he invited me to follow him there, which I did. He let me sleep on the floor of his small student flat for a few days. He seemed straight and politically on the far left and we got on with each other.

One day we travelled to Padua for a huge political demonstration against the Italian state for the arrest of Antonio Negri. Even though at that time I dint know who Antonio Negri was, I decided to go with him. Then I found out that Antonio Negri was a professor of political science at the University of Padua and he had been arrested because the state believed he had a political link with the *Brigate Rosse* / Red Brigade, that he was in fact their intellectual leader.

We went to Milano Central Station and from there to Padua. The train was packed with thousands of young people, mainly student types, converging onto this city. Soon I lost my friends, but nevertheless I decided to follow the demonstration.

This was a tense moment for Italy's history post second world war; the *Partito Democratico Cristiano* / Christian Democratic Party were kept in power by the USA's foreign intervention policies. The police and the army were pointing guns at us and searching everyone against a wall. For the first time I felt a gun pressing firmly into my back while a policeman searched me, for weapons or just because he could.

Anyway I had met new people at the demonstration who I followed to Venice the same night. I guess it was late February or March 1979.

Venice was 2 city stops from Padua. We slept in the station. Venice was fully covered by fog. I couldn't see more than 2 feet away from me. It was kind of magical, mesmerising, a beautiful place, and being still winter it was not as busy as it usually becomes in spring.

I remained in Venice for over 2 months. I usually slept on the steps of San Marco's library with my sleeping bag, especially during March and early April, with some other people. One could say we were travellers, rather than homeless or tramps. Most people passed through, coming and going. They would usually be around for few days, maximum a week, then gone without trace, often without saying goodbye.

From Easter Venice got much busier with visitors / tourists. Piazza San Marco especially was super busy with people and pigeons everywhere. I survived by begging for money, mainly in the daytime, saying that I wanted to go back home but dint have enough money to buy myself a train ticket.

Overall, the passing tourists were generous but sometimes the same people would bump in to me a few days later and would ask me, 'are you still here?' I would say that I still dint manage to get my ticket money yet.

I became dirty and unkempt. There was one large paying public toilet with showers but after a while I started to not bother so much as I dint have clothes to change into. But I still got some interest from local predatory homos.

Often during the night a couple of men at different times would come and visit us where we slept. They would put their hands in my sleeping bag and masturbate me or I would blow them.

During my stay in Venice, a handsome guy in his teens, 16 or 17 years old, joined us on the San Marco stairs. He had run away from home like I did and we start going around together. For a few days we were inseparable. I was desperately infatuated with him, I don't know if he knew.

One day he told me he had been invited for a dinner by one of the men that come around at night and who was living in Venice, which he went to and I never seen him again. He was gone.

As the days got hotter, I started to get a *traghetto* (little boat) to the Lido di Venezia / the Venice Lido because there were beaches, and you could sleep on the ones that were not private or owned by hotels.

I can't remember how, but I managed to find myself a job while I was there. My job was painting the cabins on some of the beaches on the Lido for 4,000 lire per day.

I also made friends with this guy in Venice who was selling second hand left-wing political and philosophical books under the arches of San Marco Square without a permit. Sometimes he had to get his books fast and run.

He was living in a small flat in the poorest area of Venice, at the far back after the Arsenale and *i giardini* / the gardens, where every morning when the laguna was rising it would flood the houses and flats with shit and black dirty smelly water. One day he brought me to see one of the ghettos where the poorest people were living: it was dark, squalid and stinky I remember, but I liked it.

It was very early in the month of May, one Sunday, when my stay in Venice drastically ended. I remember I was in San Marco Square, it was around 9 or 10 in the morning, and a flag raising ceremony happening in Piazza San Marco was getting crowded. There were many tourists following this ceremony. As a navy band finished playing the ritual of raising the Italian flag along with 2 San Marco flags there was a pause and then the tourists clapped and everyone seemed happy. But then I started to clap at them too and, stupidly of me, brought attention of some policemen who arrested me for insulting the flag.

I was at the police station for half a day and then they give me a piece of official paper that stated that I had been banned from the City of Venice for the minimum of 2 years for being undesirable. I was given 24 hours to get out or face being arrested.

They also gave me a piece of paper that I could present at the train ticket office which would give me a ticket for travelling back to where I was originally registered, where my family lived. But this ticket was not free; eventually my family would get a request to pay it back, which I remember I was amused by.

When I think of Franko, I think of family, the family I never
had. We spoke the same language, literally. Italian I mean.
I'd lost my mother from cancer. He'd lost his mother being
abandoned. Now there was AIDS. We were up against the tide.
I played my mother's scarred naked corpse dragged over a
pile of rubble, over rocks, till my skin shredded. Franko
had himself filmed hurt, bleeding, punched, kicked, sliced,
stitched and brutalised. I hated to see him hurt. He exuded
longing to be loved. He was always in love. We had this
affinity. I loved 'im half a life time, for a life line. Oh
holy mother! That's almost 30 years our lives did cross.

Anna Thew, artist and teacher

Franko B is one of the most iconic performance artists
of his generation. An actionist, activist, painter and
provocateur — and a survivor to boot — Franko is unique
among his peers for the vital strength of his work and
the power of his conviction, which manifest not least in
his indefatigable capacity to surprise his audiences by
requiring us to serially reimagine and understand what he
does as an artist — and how. He refuses to stay still or to
allow his provocations to take an expected, comfortable or
conforming shape.

Dominic Johnson, writer

So I left Venice. Of course I left, but I dint go to Cascina La Ca / Lesmo, which would have meant my mother, but back to Como. I went to Donatella and she was happy to see me, saying she was hoping that I would stay a bit and work again in the restaurant. But I dint. I was ready to leave Italy, especially with the national army services looming, but first I wanted to visit my Auntie Domenica and other uncles and aunties at Gardone Val Trompia where my mother came from. And also I wanted to see my mother.

Part of the reason was that I had questions about my father to ask them all. I was hoping that now maybe someone would tell me who he was or the truth about him (what little they knew I mentioned in the early pages of this writing).

So I got the last bit of money that Donatella was looking after for me from my final leaving settlement at the pizzeria (about 200 million lire which was not bad for me) and from Como I got a train to Novara and then my uncle Aldo came to get me and bring me to San Nazzaro Sesia, where I remained for a couple of days.

While I was at my Auntie Domenica's I borrowed a bicycle from my uncle and decided to visit Biandrate, no more than 5-6 kilometres from San Nazzaro Sesia. More than Biandrate, I somehow wanted to see Fernando (yes, that Fernando – the one that bullied me to give him my mother's money and the same one who then come to the Red Cross Institute).

I don't know why I thought it would be a good idea but I did, so I went to his old house which I found very easily in the derelict housing estate. It was almost 9 years since I had been in this town or seen his house.

One of his sisters told me that he was at a particular bar in the town so I went to find him. The bar was very empty, except for 2 people, a man and a woman in their late teens. I immediately recognised him but I dint know her and so I say 'Fernando?' He stares at me but with no emotion and no answer, so I leave them and go back to my auntie's house.

I was a bit sad about Fernando not responding to me but I got over it quickly.

After Fernando blanked me, it reconfirmed that I had to run away from Italy.

I went to see my Uncle Antonio (Toni) and Giorgio, the uncles I was most bonded with. Last time I seen them was during the wedding, almost 5 years before. I spent 2 weeks in Gardone Val Trompia.

Uncle Toni was a lumberjack and I remember how in those two weeks I would go with him to collect and cut wood. Once the wood was cut, it was sent downhill with a rope. While there I told him I wanted to leave and he wasn't happy about it. He asked me not to do it and said that I could stay and work with him for a bit if I wanted.

His niece was a pretty girl that I found out had a crush on me; once she knew I wanted to leave she hid my ID card. She dint want me to go, and in those two weeks we had a kind of platonic love story. We slept together in the same bed with her little brothers and sisters... I recall some nights me and her would hide under the sheets, kissing each other... I felt very close to her very quickly, though we were second cousins and this stopped us going any further.

The day before I was leaving, my cousin finally confessed to me that she loved me. I guess she told me she loved me because she wanted me to stay, but it was a crazy idea, it would have been a scandal. Although one night we got very near fucking and it was only because the kids were in our bed that we dint do it. They saved us.

Next, in Como, I went to Donatella to collect the last of my savings, which was about 100,000 lire, then I went to my friend that had my Vespa scooter and sold it to him for 150,000 lire. I remember I gave 50,000 lire to a heroin friend that always thought that I wanted his dick, though I never did... I just loved him.

That night I slept in the bench of a park in Como. I was disturbed by 2 fascists but they dint beat me up.

The following morning I met Mario, my friend from Cantù who used to work with me as a dish washer (he was my only friend really by this time) as we had planned our travel out of Italy together.

Mario and I had 2 different agendas on why we wanted to leave Italy. He wanted just to go to Amsterdam / Holland, to buy some acid and then come back to Italy to sell it for profit. For me, it was different; it was an excuse to run away from Italy, mainly to avoid the military service. Mario dint have this problem because his Dad was dead and for this reason he was excluded because he had to provide for his family.

So the idea was to hitchhike to Holland via the north east of Italy: Val D'Aosta through France then Holland. But there was a technical problem to surpass - the border between Italy and France. I had to show my identity card but it was not valid for leaving Italy because of my age, and because my military service was pending. Of course I knew this so I did scratched out the sentence printed on the back of my identity card that was said that it was not valid outside Italy / *'questo document non e'valido per l'estero'*.

Once at the Italian / French border, the border control patrol realised what I had done and dint let me pass. In fact, he told me off for trying and said that I was lucky not to get arrested for it.

So back at square one, a few kilometres away from the border, Mario suggested I try to exit the Italian border in a goods truck as the police usually would not check the identity of the truck driver (it was not their job but the job of the *Guardia di Finanza* / Customs and Excise).

I don't know how Mario knew this, but he was right. We truck we got on went direct to a special reserved area where customs guards had an office to process the goods. The driver then went into the office with the paperwork for his cargo, and as long I stayed in the truck and the documents and papers were deemed to be in order he would be allowed to carry on his journey and so would I.

It worked!! Half an hour later I was in France outside the Mont Blanc tunnel waiting for Mario to come through.

That night, we slept in an abandoned shed. Most of the time we would eat cheese and bread and drink beer. During the trip I realised that Mario was intolerant of certain specific topics, especially the fact that I was now open with him about being gay. (He was a bloody bigot.) We would sleep in sheds, grass, fields. One night we were settling down in a forest for the night and we had this strong feeling that someone was observing us, so we decided to leave the place. It wasn't a pleasurable feeling.

Once in Le Havre or Dieppe – I can't remember which one – Mario and I were ready to go to Holland after two weeks in France. Though we realised that we dint have enough money to travel, least of all to buy what we had intended to at the beginning of our trip. So, because the trip to England was cheaper and quicker than to Holland, we planned to go to London, buy some LSD there and then go to the Isle of Wight where one of Mario's brothers had worked before.

The 18th of June '79, we took the ferry to England. Once we arrived, the police asked me to fill in a form where I should have stated the reason of my travelling. I wrote I was a student and I was on my holiday, so after checking my rucksack and my ID (the same one that dint allow me to cross the French borders) they let me in.

The reason why the English police let me cross the borders I presume was because at that time the Italian government used to stamp the back of the ID, and of course it was in Italian, so as my ID was in a documents bag and also was written in Italian, and scratched, the police wouldn't have been able to read it.

First thing we did, as soon as the train reached London, was to go to Piccadilly and try to buy some acid. Mario knew about some of these things because his brother had been through London before and said you could buy drugs in Piccadilly and on the Kings Road.

It was not long before a tall man that reminded me of a Native American approached us. He was a dealer apparently. Mario, with his poor English (and me with none of it) told him what we were after, and then he left and come back after an hour. He gave us a little bag with green pills inside, and Mario and I started to think of how to reach the Isle of Wight.

We started walking towards Wimbledon and eventually found the motorway thanks to a guy who had joined us in order to show us the right way. He was a pretty tall guy, American and a basketball player, or this is what he said to us.

The strength required to rebuild your life having survived childhood abuse is staggering. To be able to rebuild your life and go on to make profound and genre defining art, is beyond words or admiration. Franko does this repeatedly and consistently, with beauty, anger, tenderness and a righteous fuck you to those with power. To have the scars of our collaboration on my skin, to see them everyday, is a huge privilege.

the vacuum cleaner, artist and activist

Franko is that special mixture of compassion and real care for the human condition, with something very gentle at his core.

His contradictions though are powerful and become harnessed in his practice.

He draws from an interior life, memories and imaginings, with a deep sense of agency – an underground which is more difficult, darker, risky.

The body as site, at times strong and toxic both- whitened baby like or bleeding as a martyr within the church of catholic guilt.

There is a seriousness matched by purpose, risks faced to find freedoms, a preparedness to step beyond what is known, an artist to be.

Nigel Rolfe, artist

While by the motorway we decided to try one of the acid pills Mario bought in Piccadilly. It seemed to us that these dint work so well, so after a while we took another one. After our third attempt we suddenly realised that the dealer in Piccadilly gave us fake acid.

Somehow we managed to reach the Isle of Wight. Once we found the hotel, Mario went inside and as he was the only one who could speak some English, asked for a job. But, I guess because of our condition – dirty, stinky and weird – we were told there was no job available.

At that point we were absolutely skint. No money whatsoever. We started knocking at some door asking for money in order to buy something to eat. We managed to buy some eggs and a tin of baked beans and once we cut the tin in two we cooked the eggs inside.

We were now stuck on the island for a week as we dint have the money to get the boat back to the mainland. The ticket was just under 4 pounds each, so we started asking for money outside a pub. One man in his late 50s approached us, asking what our problem was. We managed somehow to explain that we were collecting money to go back to London. The guy was really nice to us, invited us inside the pub where he was with his wife, and paid for us to have drinks and some chips. Then he gave us a place to sleep in his caravan and the following day he gave us the money to buy the fare for the boat back to the mainland.

Once on the mainland we went back to London. In order to survive, we went to the West End, Piccadilly, Green Park, Bond Street etc... etc... as there were lots of Italian restaurants and we thought we would have a better chance to ask for food or help. Some of the restaurants were nice, they would give us some bread or a plate of pasta and even advise us how to survive in London.

We slept in parks, gardens and in some public toilets that were open 24 hours.

I can't recall how long it had already been since we were back in London, but one morning I woke up with a terrible toothache. I walked to Bond

Street and got into the first restaurant I seen (La Vecchia Milano) and asked for food and help.

I was told then that one of their restaurants, around the corner in Dover Street (in fact part of the same restaurant chain, under the name of 'Spaghetti House'), was looking for a dishwasher in their kitchen for the day. If I wanted I could go there and work for a day, and afterwards they would bring me to a dentist or dental hospital.

Once I finished working, someone brought me to UCL Hospital in Goodge Street. The dentist took out three teeth and gave me some antibiotics.

The manager of the restaurant where I just did those hours offered me the job, permanently. The wage was 48 pounds per week, and he could rent me a shared room for 9 pounds a week.

I accepted!!!

The restaurant La Trattoria del Cacciatore was in Dover Street and it was a first class restaurant apparently. It was usually full of rich people, MPs from the Conservative Party, and once even Lady Di come to eat there, while Rod Stewart would come once in a while with a different top model every time.

Tony was the manager at this branch of the restaurant chain Spaghetti House and not all their restaurants were first class... He was from Sicily and he liked me and took care of me. He was also my landlord; I lived in one of 2 houses in north west London that he was letting shared rooms in. I was in Ealing. (Mario had found a job as a dish-washer in a posh north African club / restaurant on Piccadilly where also they had live music and belly dancers.)

In the restaurant where I was working most of the staff were from Italy, with a few Portuguese. I would work 5 days a week, from 9.30am to 3pm, to then come back at 6.30pm and finish at 11pm.

I think that I lost contact almost immediately with Mario and I dint even know where he was staying. The only thing I remember is that I seen him twice more and he said he wanted to go back to Italy, which I assumed he must have done.

I was happy there. I felt free by now. I was a punk; in fact an *Italian* punk in *London*, and I was colouring my hair with food colouring and henna as I dint know where to find proper Crazy Colour dye (eventually I did find some in Carnaby Street).

I could not speak English but via the restaurant and Spaghetti House and the West End I would meet many Italian people. I made friends with some of them, especially 2 who were working at one of the Spaghetti House restaurants and living in the same one of Tony's houses that I was living in.

They were in England, I discovered, just for the summer, mostly because they wanted to go to the Magic Mushrooms Festival in Wales in September. I decided therefore, when September come, I had to go with them too. So in mid September 1979 I left the restaurant to go to Wales.

Tony, my manager, was cool about it. He thought I was crazy but I was young so he told me that if I made it back to London and needed a job I should come to him and he would give me back my job and a place to sleep.

The Magic Mushrooms Festival was in the middle of nowhere, somewhere in Wales. The nearest village / town was Devil's Bridge, where there was just one pub and a very old train station. As soon as I and the other two guys got into the pub, we realised that the people inside were talking another language.

We asked them if they knew where the site of the festival was. They refused to speak English to us, and now maybe I realise they were not that friendly because they were not happy about people getting off their heads going around fields looking for magic mushrooms, but eventually somebody pointed out to us that it was about 3-5 kilometres outside the village.

About 1 kilometre before we reached the actual site, a few guys we had seen some kilometres before (and I assumed had been going to the same festival as us as they looked like bikers) stopped us. We realised that they were police officers looking quite ragged. They checked our documents, and the car, and when they realised we were clean, they let us go. In that period the 'magic' mushrooms were actually legal (it only became illegal to supply them in the UK in 2005).

94

The festival site was an open field about the size of a proper football pitch. It consisted of a small stream, and spread everywhere: tents, cars, vans (hippy style), and motorbikes. It looked like a Native American camp similar to those in the western movies. So the people who inhabited the place... some of them looked very old, though young... and vice versa.

There seemed to be many people there, maybe up to 200. The day after we arrived, me and the 2 Italian travel companions started looking for the magic mushrooms... it wasn't so difficult. To find them we just walked in fields and started eating them as we were picking them up from the earth.

Only when night fell did we realise that we were far from the camp, so, semi-high and in the dark, we started walking back until we heard someone speaking English. The thing was that we could hear voices, but we couldn't see anybody... then we started making noises... until the voices become blood and flesh as Mary and Steve from the camp, back from the small village after finding some milk. Thanks to them we were able to get back to our tent and to come back to conscious status after sharing the milk with Mary and Steve. Apparently milk helps stop the effect of the mushrooms.

Mary and Steve took us to their tent that was close to another one where Mary's son Todd and his mostly punk friends, Tim and Noel, were. They were all in their teens.

After introducing myself, we started to spend more and more time together and completely forgot about the Italian guys, until I realised they had left the festival and took the tent because it was theirs, but the weird thing is I don't remember where I was actually sleeping then. Also I don't remember saying goodbye to them.

I think that I was too high all the time there, I was like a kid in sweet shop, except the mushrooms were free. The only thing I remember of that festival was that I dint really have a sense of day or night and I would wake up in different places in different tents... once even in the stream...

How long was I there? No real idea... Maybe 1 week or 10 days but I remember when I left most people and caravans and tents had gone. I had spent most of the time there practically eating just mushrooms and I lost at least 1 stone from either vomiting or shitting.

On my way back to London, on my own and by lots of walking (for 3 days out of Wales; nobody would stop for me) I had a lift from this man in his late 40s-50s, who picked me up before the city of Oxford.

He was English but he could speak good Italian. He offered me food at a Little Chef on some motorway. He asked me to go to the bathroom and wash myself, my hands and face. After the lunch break, he took me to the edge of London.

Once in London I went to see Tony, my ex work manager and landlord. While waiting on the tube I met an Italian couple who were living in one of Tony's places. I recognised them, yet maybe because I was still high or spaced out when they approached me I freaked out on them.

Anyway eventually I spent two days with them, before moving back in as a shared room tenant in one of Tony's houses.

I was a punk rocker working in a first class restaurant. When Tony gave me back my job at restaurant, he would warn me when the owners of the Spaghetti House chain were coming to visit.

I remember how one day two of the owners, who coincidently originally come from a small place near the Red Cross Institute in Mergozzo where I had spent my childhood, did not bother me about my appearance as soon as they found out I was from the Red Cross. Actually they had sympathy for me, although they had reservations about me being seen by the posh clientele. I was most of the time in the kitchen, nevertheless Tony would stand up for me if people asked why he had a punk rocker as worker. He would say that I was reliable and a good worker.

I had got back to London and got myself sorted out, so I started to pay visits to Noel and Tim and Todd, the 3 boys I met at the Magic Mushrooms camp. Before I had left the festival, they had asked me to go and visit them.

They lived in Brixton, in a squat, and I would also meet Steve and Mary again and meet some of the inner circle of family / friends / children. But I became very close to Noel and Tim and I would see them at least 3-4 days a week after work. I ended up spending more time sleeping at their flat than at Tony's house.

97

My English was improving, and I soon realised that I was the only one who had a permanent job. For Noel, when he needed money urgently, he worked as a rent boy and would visit some gentleman's clubs around Westminster to raise some cash. Tim was the younger – maybe 17 years old – and was coming to terms with some stressful episode back home with his family, somewhere in North London. One of his older brothers, Bryan, lived in the squat next door with some rockers.

I was taking drugs most times when I went round to Noel and Tim's house. LSD and acid to amphetamine and methadone and barbiturates. One time I remember about 1week before Christmas, after work, I went to Brixton to Noel and Tim's and we decided to buy some methadone from one of Tim's brother's housemates next door. We paid 50p for a shot and drank it; I only recall how sick I was all night long.

Nevertheless in the morning I was supposed to go to work, but because I was very, very sick eventually in the early evening of that day I decided to go back to Tony's house in Ealing.

While at Hammersmith tube station, a group of football supporters passed by. It was Saturday and, well, it was a common thing during the football season to see them around, especially drunk and noisy. As soon as they noticed me, they jumped into the carriage I was sitting in, and started beating me up because I was a dirty punk.

They kicked and punched me to the floor, beating me while a couple of them was keeping the door of the train open. Eventually they jumped off and the train just moved on.

What kind of shocked me was the fact that some of the passengers in the same carriage with me prior to the attack, they just got up and moved along to the next section of the open carriage. This was shocking to me and hurt more than the beating, although I did loose 3 teeth.

What provoked them? Because I was a punk, with pink hair, and fake leopard trousers with a skirt on top?

Anyway when I got to my stop at Ealing, the ticket controller dint even bother to ask me if I had the ticket, as my face was bloodied and blue. Once Tony seen me, he gently rebuked me, saying that I'd better think about my future, and then he tended to me and took care of me.

A few days later I went back to Brixton and Noel saw my face was still bruised. He suggested to me to start a kung fu course so I would be able to protect myself and also because he had also had trouble with football fans because of the way he was looking.

So we started it in January 1980, at Crystal Palace. The master was a crazy man called Jacob. In the course there were loads of hetero men, others were police officers, and then there was Ivan, a very pretty boy skinhead. He was utterly gorgeous, but I had still a crush on Noel (Noel was not so bothered about my sexual interest in him but was nice to me. For sure he was fucking Tim, Todd *and* had eyes on Ivan). By now I was open about my sexuality. If people asked I would be honest about it and if they dint like it they should not have asked me in the first place.

In January 1980, before my 20th birthday, I finally officially moved to Brixton with Noel and Tim (the house was busy with people visiting / staying, punks and queers after some punk gigs or parties. All the time I would come home from work and there would be some cute boy in my room / bed inviting me to join him).

For about 6 months we stayed in this house on the top of Railton Road towards Herne Hill, I think the number was 253, on the corner of Mayall Road, then we got an eviction order. The house was the property of Lambeth Council who wanted it back.

Noel, Tim and I squatted another flat about 200 yards down the same road, in the middle of the 'Infamous Front Line' (the frontline of the Brixton Riots in 1981), in a housing block of 20 flats called St George's Residence. They belonged to the council (apart from 3 flats that were in private hands) and were inhabited by nuns till the early 60s, before the Jamaican diaspora.

The apartment was in the mezzanine over three floors, and it was completely run down and mostly without electricity. Our new flat was number 7, on the first floor, and each apartment had 2 bedrooms.

The same night we moved there, I remember it was summer 1980 and was particularly hot, and I decided to leave the windows open and went to sleep. A knife on my throat woke me up; there were three men, probably dealers, that were looking for the previous occupants who I think left in a hurry because of heroin dealing and taking.

They forced us to sit in one bed and covered us with the duvet, in the meantime giving Noel especially a lot of light hammer blows to his body and head, asking him where we had hidden the drugs... Somehow, after a while, another guy come into the apartment and when he seen us he recognised that we were not the people they were looking for, so they left, without forgetting to take all the little money we had and our cigarettes.

The following week police come to our flat. They were looking for the same people. While in the flat the officers seen some of my gay porno images on my room wall and they told me this material was illegal, even though since they were from the drug department they dint bother me more.

Besides those two unwanted visits, our apartment was always busy with people coming in and out. Our recreational time would shift from having sex to taking drugs, mostly with friends that Noel had attracted.

Once a French guy called Bertrand come to the flat. He spent three or four days with us and he was astonishingly gorgeous. Noel and I had sex with him, and actually I had a crush on him and when he left I longed for him to come back. After a few years we received a letter from his sister telling us that Bertrand had lost an eye after being attacked by a group of fascist skinheads in Paris.

Brixton wasn't the suburban middle class residency of the 50s anymore, but mostly the West Indies population that moved in the end of British colonisation and the aftermath of World War Two from countries like Jamaica, Dominican Republic, Trinidad and others that came to Britain to work on the buses, NHS, and other public areas. The Brixton of the 60s and 70s come to be seen more as a ghetto and most of the whites that lived there were either really poor, hippies, punks, or middle-class liberals. Brixton was full of squatters and occupied houses, not so uncommon in London but the then very left wing-controlled council was known for incompetence and corruption.

But I loved Brixton and I was having a good time there. I did feel safe, at least from fascists or football fans. Brixton was poor but there was life, it was not like any other place in London that I knew of or was aware of. Yes it was poor in places but the best was that you could get on to be what you wanted to be, especially in the summer on the Front Line, always with lots of people

Franko you are a sort of angel in my life, and
an antidote to the drab, dull and heartless.
No superlatives are super enough.

Marcia Farquhar, artist

These stories of Franko's childhood that I know, including
the ones that legend have bent, color my experience of
his work. I've been in it for a long ride, 22 years. We have
a long-love. I heart-feel the language he uses, yes it
can be relentlessly harsh or shamelessly sappy. There's
impossible damage, the Loved will have started Unloved.
I'm scraped, humored, and touched.

Ron Athey, artist

I met Franko in 1983 as an aspiring artist, gay and an anarchist – what a beautiful alchemy! Always outspoken, passionate to the extreme for the rights of animals and people and have the fondest memories of hanging out, agitating, and being arrested together!

Phil Stebbing , film maker

Franko B, I often find myself wishing he'd been my brother. It would certainly have made my family a lot more interesting. His uncompromising integrity, his bravery, his complete disregard for fashion, his refusal to conform, his unique voice... Uncle Keith would have met his match at the turgid family Christmases. That's for sure.

Anthony Roberts, producer

on the street chanting, singing, dancing, openly smoking marijuana with loud reggae and blues parties blasting out of people's houses / cars / shops / pubs that played ska, punk, reggae, jazz, rock, Latin American music...

There was a brilliant, independently run cinema called The Ritzy which showed independent films with all-night events. The theme varied to try to serve the wide community, its cultural and demographic diversity.

Many people that dint live in Brixton regarded it as a no-go area for respectable people. It was a ghetto but it dint have the mentality of a ghetto.

Not all London was cool; there were places that were dangerous (I suppose like anywhere in the world). You could pop up in different area with its own factions.

Working around Italian people and meeting a lot of them that were working for Spaghetti House, more and more I was realising how Italians in London who had lived there for years – some of the second generation in London – had created pockets of ghetto, with Italian schools, Italian churches... Some of the older guys I met that were in London for 40 years or so dint even speak English and had a very bigoted, racist and dull conservative attitude towards others that were not them or the city they were living in. In a bizarre way they were exactly like they would have been back in Italy or Portugal around issues of race, sexuality, women, etc... etc... And if they voted they were definitely voting Tory.

Not everybody at work was cool with me being what I was or what I represented to their sensibilities. The 2 Portuguese that were in the kitchen especially (the chef and second chef) were the most macho and bigoted and in the closet. They had a love and hate kind of relationship with me. They were disgusted by me but they always touched my ass and pushed their bodies against me, grabbed me in the cellar room, and one of them actually turned up once at my house in Brixton soon after his first child was born to put his cock in my mouth, probably because his wife was more busy feeding the new baby.

Anyway I did enjoy his cock and aggressive sexual energy. He thought he was topping me but he got it wrong. Of course the first thing after coming in my mouth was 'don't tell anybody or I'll kill you'. Classic! I met lots of people like that in my life, in Italy and here in London.

Being in London at that time and being a punk saved my life, as English (but especially London) freedoms towards sex, identity, and gender transgression was widely open compared to some parts of Europe, with the exception of Amsterdam. I never hung around with my work colleagues outside work, but back in Brixton, for the first time since I had left the Red Cross, I started feeling very close to a group of people and feel I was part of them and vice versa.

One of these new friends, who was living with us in the squat briefly, one day decided to run down the road (yes, the Front Line on the Railton Road) completely naked. He was sure he was the reincarnation of Jesus Christ. He was high on LSD for a few days. We dint see him again.

In Brixton very early on, I met this guy who was living next door to us with Tim's brother. Everybody called him Apache as he claimed that his family background was from the Apache tribe, though nobody was sure about it or believed him (for sure he was Canadian).

Apache would sell drugs; most of the time, speed. One night Apache shot me up with speed and we spent the night doing it and probably talking shit. Very close to dawn we began kissing and masturbating each other. Even though Apache stated lots of times he was hetero and had a girlfriend, this dint stop me, this dint bother me. By now I had had sex with more men who said they were hetero than men who identified themselves as homosexual.

One of the drawbacks of living in Brixton was that the police were much more visible in the street and they were aggressive. They dint like the blacks, the punks, the queers, the anarchists, the poor... There was a period when every time I came out of Brixton tube station I would be stopped, searched, followed, harassed – day and night.

I remember once Noel and I left the squat because we couldn't sleep; we were just walking around late at night – 2 or 3am – when suddenly 2 cars of plain clothes police officers jumped on us. The first thought was that they were some fascists looking for trouble, which they were but they were legitimised by their jobs. Their questions were 'Where the drugs? Where the weapons?' while they were physically aggressive, holding us in a headlock.

Franko B è il mio amico più tatuato che ho.
Io ce l'ho tatuato nel cuore.

Franko B is the most tattooed friend I have.
I tattooed him in my heart.

Patrizia Marras, artist

Artist, activist, animal lover,
Genius, genuine, generous,
Passionate, truthful, vulnerable.
Fighting for right(s) and battling
against wrongs.
Franko through thick and thin
a friend who is more like family.

Gill Lloyd, Producer

What Franko lacks in athleticism he makes up for in complete commitment and determination, which makes him a very popular member of The Fitzroy Lodge Boxing Club. Whether training, sparring or competing, there is never anything short of 100% effort. Franko doesn't do 'half measures'. His drive and discipline are a motivation and inspiration to all of his fellow boxers.

Steve Diggory, boxing trainer

Franko B is my favourite artist. Challenging, beautiful, funny, poetic. And his art isn't bad either.

Paddy Glackin, friend

I become much closer to Noel than Tim, and one time again I told him that I loved him. He replied he wasn't interested in any kind of romantic bond, and that he wanted to be free as always. Anyway, we ended up having some kind of sex. A day or two after we had sex together, I realised I had an infection, something similar to a herpes or some kind of STD but on my dick.

Noel brought me to St George's Hospital in Camberwell which had a sex clinic, and told me to say that I slept with a woman and not him. The doctor or nurse, who I have to say probably dint believe us, put something in my penis which really hurt, took a sample, and warned me to be more careful. After giving me some antibiotics she sent me home.

When I was not working at the kitchen I was tripping, or speeding on cheap amphetamine most of the time. Sometimes I would wear a top hat, a tuxedo that I found, probably in some charity shop, tight trousers with a skirt on top, and long shirts. I loved colouring my hair. If I have to say how many times I had dyed my hair, or cut it, I can't really remember...

Also I started to become aware that there were different type of punk movement informed by specific politics and a style that comes with that. There was the punk rock type, like the class of '76 (that by 1979 was dead for various reasons and was seen as more commercial) with figurehead bands like The Sex Pistols, The Clash, Siouxie and the Banshees, The Damned and more, then there was the punk which had a much less commercial sound and more political conscience: Bands like Crass and Poison Girls, Conflict, Flux of Pink Indians etc... etc... were more politically active against wars... They were anti-nuclear, pro-animal rights, feminism, gender benders and more.

It was in Charing Cross the first time I got into a gay club. The club was called Heaven and the owner was Richard Branson. Since our social group was against any kind of sexual discrimination, especially in a place for gays, we went there with a friend who was girl (Evelyn) who was dressed as a man, otherwise she wouldn't be able to get in. And not only was she a woman but I remember she was the only black person in the entire club.

As for the gays, they all looked the same. They were all clones, like the one in the Village People, so most of the people in the club were dressed with jeans, plaid shirts, moustaches, etc... all the same. So we stood out. After a while they found out there was a woman with us so they kicked us out.

At number 6, next to our apartment at St George's Residence, there were 2 guys living there who were also homosexual, Chris and Stan. Stan would usually sell me the diet / sleeping pills that his doctor prescribed to him. They had amphetamines in. He sold 3 pills for a pound: a bargain. They were yellow and they worked!

I came to Britain in mid-June 1979. This was less than a month after Thatcher come to power and in just under 2 years here in London I could see the change of mood and the escalation of policies designed to make the rich richer and the poor poorer.

Margaret Thatcher and her party's fascist agenda against the poorest and destitute started to bite and I could feel the uncertainty everywhere. Communities all around Britain were victimised and strategically made to fail because they dint vote for this regime. Brixton was one of the communities at the receiving end of these policies, which manifested in high unemployment, lack of employment prospects, and police aggression and brutality, which eventually brought discontent and riots to the streets of Brixton.

I think this extraordinary climax was a reflection of policies of harassment against such communities and there was evidence (and not just rumour) that the police were raiding local shops, clubs, bars, community centres and youth clubs that were owned or serviced by the black communities in Brixton.

Also I could not help noticing in the 6 months prior to the riots, the increased presence of a police unit called SPG (Special Patrol Group). Basically they just went around, sometimes in unmarked vans, intimidating and provoking the community I was living in. Many times in the middle of the day or night they would come up to you on the road and just slowly move you along.. I had it done to me and I have seen this subtle technique done to others, especially on the Front Line.

One day, in early April 1980, the people of Brixton said 'enough is enough'.

I remember it was a grey Saturday morning. I went to town to work at the restaurant about 9am and there where hundreds of police with dogs lining up from my house on 224 Railton Road to the tube station in Brixton.

By the time I come back to the same station at around 4pm there were more police all over the centre of Brixton and hundreds of people ready to kick off.

As the trouble started and turned into a riot I was asked by someone that knew of me to give away leaflets to people in the street, about free legal advice and what to do if they got arrested: phone numbers, your rights, witnessing etc... etc... The police had people taking photos of everyone, including observers and people like me that were not causing trouble but helping distribute vital advice.

Nobody knows who started the riot, though the clashes between the people and the officers carried on for a few days, with pauses at night, and then it would start again in another corner of Brixton's community. Buildings were set on fire, burglaries, and police charging, protesters... Towards the end of the riot the police forces were almost in their thousands, with more busloads of police officers brought in from all over the country.

The first 2-3 days, for about 2 weekends, the trouble focused on the Front Line almost exactly in front of St George's Residence, my house. A few months earlier we had become a housing co-op certificated by Lambeth Council and managed to put a gate in front of our courtyard. This become useful during the riot because technically the police could not trespass; it was the private property of the co-op which had the apt name of Front Line Housing Co-op. It meant that we could rescue people that were running away from the street and protect them from the clutches of the police. Also our residence become a first aid point for injured people that happened to be on the street during the riot.

Of course the police dint like this. In the weeks following the riot they were trying to find out information that would have incriminated us. Detectives came around and asked questions to the neighbours and us, asking if anybody was involved in the actual riot... could we give names? But we were not and dint give names.

It was in this period exactly that I came across and got involved with the 121 anarchist bookshop that was 100 yards across the road from St George's Residence.

Margaret and Peter, an Australian couple with a young child that were living in one of the flats in our block, were involved in running this anarchist centre / bookshop. After the riot I became more conscious and involved in anarchic political activism – against any kind of state-led oppression – and started frequently volunteering to keep the bookshop open a couple times per week after work.

In the anarchism ideology, for me, I find the closest thing to my idea of freedom. Just being a punk was not enough no more. To just say 'fuck off' was not enough no more. To just be angry was not enough no more.

This awareness changed my attitude towards my everyday life: I started somehow to see Noel and Tim less and less, also because they were not particularly interested in being politically or socially involved.

I had become vegetarian and we organised, every Friday, a dinner for 1 pound as a way to come together and discuss and meet people that were interested and believed in a better world. I was an idealist and an optimist now; I believed that we could fight the power. As I say, I was an idealist.

The anarchist centre also gave advice to people on squatting, human rights, nuclear disarmament, race, work, promoted anti-war materials and anti-apartheid, and demonstrated against any kind of oppression. I remember that for a period after the riot on Saturday afternoon every week for a while we would have an open meeting where anybody could come and meet and share information and experiences.

In May 9181, during one of these open meetings, I met someone called Tom V. Tom V was 4 years older than me, a medical researcher with a Marxist brother called Ed, and a girlfriend. I fell desperately in love with him. Next time I seen him I expressed my feelings to him. He replied he wasn't gay.

In the meantime a flat had come free on the ground floor of our block and Margaret and Peter asked me if I wanted to move in. My life at number 7 with Tim and Noel was no longer compatible. Tim especially had some personal traumas that he was not able to talk about or get help for and he was becoming more reclusive and anti-social. Noel was becoming a Hare Krishna follower. The place was always filthy till I cleaned and the day after would be exactly the same, so I moved out and on.

At first I shared the flat downstairs with Jessica, a friend and anarchist also involved with the anarchist bookshop. She shared the 2 bedroom flat with me for 2 months, and then she moved around the corner with one of her boyfriends. I stayed there for 14 years.

About my first romantic and platonic story so to speak (with Tom V, the medical researcher): it lasted more than 25 years (we are still very good friends even if we only see each other 3 or 4 times a year). I was infatuated at first, then madly in love with him, after he come to my flat a few days following our first encounter on the Saturday afternoon at the 121 anarchist centre. When I told Tom V that I loved him, he had said he liked me but he was not gay... but then said he wasn't so against the idea of having *something*.

He told me that he never actually had a sex with a man but that he nearly did with someone he once knew that he really liked and had grown up with, but when they arranged a date to potentially get off with each other his friend dint turn up and so it was left at that.

I believed Tom V; I dint have any reason not to. A few nights later, Tom V and a few other friends and I went back to the club Heaven. This time the club was mixed and the music was better than 1 year before. After we left the club, Tom V decided to spend the night around mine. And we started kissing and masturbating. I remember that the following morning, just before leaving, he told me that he liked me and that it was lovely but I shouldn't expect more than this.

After a week I met him again, he told me that he had spoken with his girlfriend (later the mother of his 3 lovely kids) about what had happened between us, he told me that she told him that I was going to get hurt and that he should be careful of what he was doing. I could see her point but in the long run I actually dint get hurt – it allowed me to be free. I got over the idea to be with Tom V in a monogamous way.

Broken language from a torn being who must speak, must keep opening up his flesh to live. A fugitive life, running through and from the careless, violent world; loving, fucking, giving, taking, leaving again, burning... all distilled in art's remaking. Where the vital edges of sense and experience are, there you'll find Franko B.

Adrian Heathfield, curator and writer

Franko is beautiful, kind, exciting, gentle. I have known him since 1981 and our friendship has been strong and true. I am very lucky to have been so close to someone so special.

Tom V, friend

This is what then happened for about 25 years or so: we would meet about 3 to 5 times a year 'for a drink' in the earlier days, kissed and masturbated passionately, but never fucked – Tom V never wanted it and I was happy with this as it was a very special situation.

While I just got on with different sexual encounters and relationships and life in general, Tom V stayed with his then off-and-on girlfriend till she got pregnant with his first of 3 kids, which cemented their relationship for the rest of his, and her, lives.

I think this defined our 'love story', and I'm not saying this with any regrets or bitterness. I still have a lot of love for Tom V as an old friend that also many times helped me financially when in total dire need / situations, till very recently.

In 1983, after two years of involvement and commitment with the 121 anarchist bookshop / centre in Brixton, and different marginal anti-capitalism and establishment groups / activities with my fellow 'comrades', I had a falling out with essentially what was a group of pseudo-liberal middle class white people.

I started asking myself why are there not more openly LGBT or black people involved, or who want to get involved? Why was I experiencing patronising homophobia, sexism and racism? Where was the anarchist utopia gone? Why was taking drugs anti-anarchistic but smoking pot and getting stupidly drunk to get laid was not? Why was my sexuality seen by some of my fellow anarchist comrades as a bourgeois disease?

A year before I had formed a gay anarchist group. That dint really work out. There were 4 of us: me, an old man that identified himself as a paedophile, and 2 separatist lesbians. It occurred to me that all this was totally a contradictory and dysfunctional idea of what I thought being an anarchist was. Because, perhaps naively, I believed that everybody could be decent and fair to each other.

As I was struggling with this I felt isolated and patronised. So I decided to become more practical, without knowing at that time that I had become a constructive anarchist. I realised that I could not change the world or people or even try to, but I could try to live my life with dignity and integrity and purpose as much as I could.

I was 23 and I realised that this was a good moment to have a reality check and to never judge a book by its cover so to speak, that I need to have a life outside rhetoric and escapism, whether that was by drug-taking or not confronting the fact that I dint have any hold on my life. I tried to sum up what I had and besides my job at the Spaghetti House, what had I achieved? I remember I felt as if I was stripped of everything that I had or had come to believe and it was replaced for a few months by a very deep and dark – almost nihilistic – existential depression.

One day during this period I met this girl who was living a couple of streets away, very close to my place. I recalled her often riding a bike. On this day our eyes made contact and she stopped and asked me who I was, my name. Her name was Susan.

I told her all the recent happenings in my life, that my life dint have any real purpose or meaning at that moment, that I was just on a big run but I could not grasp from what I was running from, and also why bother running?

To cut it short, I dint know what to do with my life and she suggested I go with her to a ceramic course in Brixton that the local authority was running for adults. It would cost me just a pound per year and I could go there 2-3 times a week. Because I dint know what to do, and I just made a friend, I decided to have a go.

The ceramic course was held in the evenings, from 7 to 10pm, and was just meant for adults who were working daytimes, although you were allowed to go during the day, when it was mostly attended by elders or housewives who were doing ceramics as a hobby. There was also a separate school for Saturday classes in Dulwich.

After a while I started going, not just with Susan in the evening, but in the morning by myself when I was not working. One of the teachers was a guy called Keith; he was so good to me and a great tutor. After a year of attending the classes, he suggested I to go to art school and apply for a foundation course at Camberwell School of Art. Which I did, with Keith's guidance and support.

I was beginning to see that art was an important part of my life - an inseparable part of my life – where I could be myself and use the only thing that nobody, no institution, no state, could take away from me: language. Language that I had become aware that I had and that I could use to empower myself, and that, with time, this language would develop.

I don't remember exactly, around 1983/ 84, I had my first visit to a major museum in England, Tate Britain. I don't remember much of that day at Tate apart from being taken into one room by a friend. This room seemed to have a different light, atmosphere and feeling from the other rooms in the museum. The pictures at first all felt that they were out of focus and the room felt like it was immersed in some mist.

It turned out that this room was inhabited by one artist's work only, Mark Rothko. I had never heard of Rothko and to be honest I dint really know much about any art and artists then - especially 20th century ones.

I also dint know at that time what a gallery space should be like, but this felt more like being in a church or an Italian cemetery than a gallery.

In the middle of the room there were some simple benches that I could sit on and be in front of the paintings I wanted to look at by just sliding down on the bench and turning to the work I wanted to look at. I gradually shuffled my body along the bench until I had spent time looking at all of them. Just walking up to them for me was too abstracted and I felt I could not focus on them that way, but from a bit of a distance they felt like religious paintings that one might find in a church.

Eventually my friend left the room without saying anything and I just found myself alone and emotional in the space with Rothko's works.

I don't know how long I was there for - it could have be just 20 minutes or 2 hours - or whether anybody else actually came in during this time, but I felt I was lost, or found, in some magical space that I could not quantify or make sense of except by embracing it like a child would embrace his loving parents. In this moment I did find myself moved to tears by the very special space that the Rothko Room at Tate Britain was, and over the years, in successive visits, it became to me a place of pilgrimage almost.

Franko talks about the monstrous and of artists having the capacity to be monsters, to de-monstrate, to show. The providence of monster and demonstrate is *monstrum* from the Latin, with its meanings of portent, omen, abnormality, other to the hegemonic 'natural order'. Through his showings of artworks – performances, sculptures, paintings, installations, stitched works, materials are manipulated into poetic and uncontrived monstrosities. To show is to be a teacher and Franko is both a great artist and a great teacher, he shows with disarming directness – as things are.

Kira O'Reilly, artist

Franko's commitment to art has been very influential to me as an artist. His use of his own body as a canvas impacted me very much. In his bleeding performances it was implicit that the artist's heart would stop beating if no one would stop the blood from flowing. Franko truly revealed to me the body as work of art.

Gilles Jobin, artist

This experience made me realise how powerful art could be. Here I was in front of a series of abstract expressionist paintings that could make me cry in sadness and in joyful ways. This moment of discovery made me think and come to the conclusion that being an artist and making art was the only way for me to be alive and to want to stay alive. This experience in the Rothko Room made me realise how serious and important art was and was going to be to me. Before this I felt that there was nothing else much left for me - not even a small light at the end of the tunnel. I was about 23 / 24 years old and felt I was coming to a dead end as far my life prospects were going to be. But in this moment of saturated desperation this felt like the light, the tiny light of hope I was looking for to try to be happy and live in a 'meaningful' way. It seemed that in a instant I had found a reason, a strategy to be and to want to stay alive because I could try to express the inexpressible using art as a language to try to somehow make sense of what I'm doing here and how this can be shared. Suddenly I felt I could be useful and contribute to the society I lived in. I realised that art was a very generous thing in many ways and I have to say that art has been very generous to me; it's important to me to share this generosity.

When I was still involved with the anarchist centre, one day I met this guy called Gus. He come in need: he had two children and the 121 centre had a database of empty properties in the borough of Lambeth compiled by pro-squatting volunteers to help people to find houses. Through research on the houses, the owners and locations, and possibly also legal help and action, we then would suggest empty properties and help people to occupy them. Sometimes we would occupy the houses first and make them accessible to the people in need.

Gus did some minicab driving but he dint have sufficient money to rent from a landlord. As the properties available on the database were not suitable for him (and his 8 year old son), I asked Gus to move into my flat with his son Luke, while the other child went to live with Gus's ex-wife. The agreement was that Gus and Luke could stay at my flat till Gus sorted out something better for both of them.

Gus was a nice man, a bit stressed out at the time with being a lone parent. I remember he was working long hours to support himself and Luke. I dint know what happened with his ex-wife (who was living in Leeds with the other child) but Gus did have a younger partner by now and briefly all 3 stayed with me. Eventually she moved out, just around the corner into another squat sharing with somebody else I knew, but Gus and Luke stayed.

His partner was a postgraduate / MA sculpture student at Saint Martin's School of Art here in London and she introduced me to another student on her course called Elspeth, a Scottish artist. We become very good friends while she was in London studying and she helped me immensely with preparing my portfolio to apply for the foundation course at Camberwell.

As drawing from a life model was very important for her work and I needed to improve my drawing to get into college, we decided to share the cost of hiring one once a week. For a while we did drawing in my living room with a model called Steve.

Through Elspeth I came across many interesting artists, and went to galleries and museums. After few months doing drawing and ceramics, I had a decent portfolio to be shown once called for an interview. I decided on three colleges: Wimbledon, St. Martin's and Camberwell. It was December 1985. Even though St Martin's dint even call me for an interview, the other two did.

With my portfolio and Keith's reference from the pottery classes I attended my first interview at Camberwell. I remember Gus drove me in his minicab with all my ceramics pieces and drawings. There were three tutors waiting for me, and once they finished looking at my portfolio they were quite impressed.

They all agreed that it would be great if I could do the course at their college, but then just before the end of the interview, one hour or so in, the programme leader asked me, in a very polite manner, if I had some mental issues that could undermine my ability to do the course or could undermine others who I was going to study with.

I replied that... no, as far as I knew I hadn't any particular problem, at least no more than anyone else I knew... I remember a nervous laugh emitting from all of us in the room.

That Franko survived abuse and neglect to
become a flourishing artist isn't what makes him
remarkable; it's his poetic alchemy of love, the
harsh beauty of his work that seduces your heart
and stabs your conscience.

Nathaniel Walters, film maker

I first heard of Franko B with his blood-letting performances
– compelling and cathartic acts, but done with a calm and
a lack of melodrama that belied what the audience was
witnessing. Smeared with white paint, his body became a
prepared canvas for the spurts, the drips and the smears of his
own blood. A larger than life personality, flashing his gold
teeth, Franko is an exuberant but authentic person who speaks
intelligently about his art, his life and his loves.

Stelarc, artist

Two weeks after the interview the director of the course called Keith and asked the same question of him, but more directly: did he know if I had ever seen a psychologist? Keith reassured him that I was ok and they offered me a place.

One thing for sure though, I had to lie about my school qualifications – O levels and A levels – as when I applied for art college the foundation courses demanded it. The secretary of the course stressed me out for at least another 6 months after I started the course, asking for my education certificates. I had to come out with loads of different excuses, such as my mother and I had an argument and so she was refusing to send them to me or the office where I had to asked for them was not responding, etc... etc... until it was too late to matter anymore...

The summer of '86, just a few weeks before starting the course at Camberwell, I had an accidental overdose on heroin, which shocked my friends. I ended up in hospital.

It was the only time in many years that I took it as I was more into amphetamine. An old junkie friend come around to use my flat to fix himself and offered me a shot but, as I was not a frequent user of heroin, what he give me was too much for my body.

Few months later I started my foundation course at Camberwell. I would walk every day to college, 6 days a week. I was supposed to sign in every day by 8am otherwise the school could cut my bursary.

Because the bursary was quite high (50 pounds per week) I decided to leave my job at the restaurant. Even though Tony was sad about it, he was happy for me that I was back studying.

In my first few months at Camberwell I realised that I was more interested in painting than ceramics so I decided to apply to do a 3 year BA at Chelsea School of Art in the Kings Road. Chelsea gave me an interview and consequently offered me a place on the fine art painting course.

As my works were quite big, I hired a van and brought them to the interview where they were evaluated by three tutors. All of them agreed; they liked my work, so when they asked me about my qualifications and education I decided not to lie. I told them that I dint have any of the requisite O level or A levels... and they told me that they were happy to accept me without having to show them.

'WTF?!' This was the reaction of my tutors and some of my classmates at Camberwell when they found out that Chelsea had offered me a place. Many people dint expect it; in fact, they had warned me not to have any high hopes about it...

In those years, especially around '83, there was a total change in the world, in the social interaction among human beings... as a virus was spreading globally.

The only information you were given was that this virus had already killed loads in the US and had started to kill people in UK and the rest of Europe too. It was HIV, or most commonly known as AIDS. As the virus spread, so the panic was spreading amongst heteros and gays.

From that year on I was forbidden to give blood, something I had been doing for many years. Strangely this ban was extended just to the gay community. Ignorance, absence of proper information, and the paranoia, had influenced everyone, even gays. Noel, for example, my ex-flatmate who had become a Hare Krishna, he would become more and more paranoid and scared. He stopped sex altogether. He wouldn't kiss anybody, not even as a sign of greeting, and this is because of the information the state and the tabloids were giving.

Very close friends of mine started to get ill and if I have to sum up that period I would say it was an emotive and depressive climax, mostly because everybody was feeling powerless before this new disease.

I don't know if I have been lucky through not being infected with HIV; I was absolutely affected by seeing friends die and the hate and disgust of people, especially through the ignorance promoted by the tabloid media and the silence of the government at that time.

In the early confusing and fearful times, some members of the medical profession, like doctors and nurses, were very insensitive and homophobic for sure - sometimes just patronising. They would ask you all sorts of

Franko ha la bellezza di un mito ancestrale.
Nel suo corpo imperfetto c'è l'unione invincibile
di potenza e tenerezza.
Sotto il suo cielo trova spazio l'Inaccettabile,
che si trasforma così nel Sublime.
Il tempo di Franko è l'eterno presente dell'amore
che si rinnova ogni giorno.
La libertà si applica solo con la disciplina.

Franko has the beauty of an ancestral myth.
In his imperfect body there is the invincible union
of power and tenderness.
Under its sky finds space the Unacceptable, which
is thus transformed into the Sublime.
Franko's time is the eternal present of Love that
is renewed every day.
Freedom applies only to Discipline.

Maurizio Coccia, curator

Through his work, Franko B cuts through the nexus of love,
pain, and intimacy that makes life difficult but worth living.
His courage has been to move beyond suffering to make stunning
performances that make us think about how we relate to each
other and to the world.

Amelia Jones, art historian, critic and curator

questions, especially about your sexual life, and if you were open and honest they would look at you in a very judgemental way, as it was your own fault if you caught some diseases because of your 'lifestyle'.

I remember on one occasion my doctor sent me to the hospital for a blood test, just in case, because I was a homosexual. At the hospital, first I had to deal with an ignorant male doctor who (without telling me) decided to screen me for everything one could have got via sexual encounters: all the types of hepatitis they could test for at that time... syphilis... HIV...

Another time I remember especially, this one nurse at Saint George's Hospital in Camberwell treated me like shit, and when he took my blood he really hurt my arm. I was obviously in discomfort and I asked him what was going on? Why so rough with me? He looked disgusted and just told me that I should have thought about that before I had done the things I did, implying that I deserved whatever I got.

At the end of the 80s I joined a group called ACT UP London. It was formed first in the US as a response to the inactivity of the Reagan administration, who just let people die because they saw AIDS as a self-inflicted 'gay plague'.

During my period at Chelsea I curated an exhibition to help fundraise for ACT UP and some of the tutors and students donated work; we did raise some money for it.

My time at Chelsea was an amazing experience, overall very good for me, impossible to quantify. Some brilliant people and teachers and some not so good people and teachers, like in the real world I suppose.

It was a place where I was first exposed to work, artists, ideas and dreams that I had not been exposed to before. I was encouraged to question myself and to be questioned and most of the time, when it was done with honesty, generosity and humility, I was able to experiment but also to take risks and to develop, not only as an artist per se, but as a human being first.

For me this was a lifesaver out of a million so to speak. I could not fuck this up, or let anybody else fuck it up for me.

In the second year at Chelsea, because of the cuts Thatcher wanted to apply to public education, such as suspending bursaries for the poor, we occupied the Chelsea building for two days.

In 1990, after 3 years, I got my BA – a first-class award. Soon after I decided to apply for postgraduate courses at the Slade and in Belfast, as both had a good reputation and their media / performance studies suited me. But I wasn't even called for an interview.

Shelagh Cluett, an artist who was the then head of sculpture at Chelsea School of Art, suggested applying to a brand new course at Byam Shaw, then an independent art school in north London, which had a postgraduate diploma she thought would suit me.

So I did and I got in.

Byam Shaw was actually a very good understated art school. I was the only postgraduate student on the alternative media course that year. It was a good year to spend there; I was very much left on my own to get on with it with the support of technical media and darkroom staff, which was useful for me.

That year I learnt to print photos in black and white and colour from slides. They had good visiting lecturers and over the year I could also invite 3 guest lecturers from outside the college, just to have one-to-one teaching.

During my postgraduate course I started clubbing more often as I had more time to have fun. I would club at least 2 times a week, mostly with my best friend Arturo. He was a beautiful man with long dreads, originally from the Dominican Republic in the Caribbean: gay, with an ex-wife and two teenage kids.

We clubbed together for about 10 years and remained good friends until his death in 2008. In those 10 years I was clubbing and also working in gay clubs and sometimes as a model for an agency that specialised in unstereotypical models. The agency was called UGLY and I would get work from them from time to time, but not consistently enough to live on.

Anyway I would club and make art, even though it is impossible for me to say how I was able to do so, as sometimes I would not stop clubbing or leave the after-club chill out for up to 4 days in a row, and then it would take me at least 2 to 3 days to recover from the comedowns. I would eventually deal with answer machine messages requesting information about my artistic practice / work.

I was working from home: my living room was my studio but at that time it was my performances that became more and more known in London and in Europe.

I dint know about performance or study it at college, but I had started to perform for the camera (in photographs and in Super 8 and 16mm films) when I was at Chelsea in the late 80s.

As I said already I went to Chelsea School of Art to study painting, but after about a year of producing lots of paintings and objects I felt that I could not paint how I felt without the work being too naïve or decorative or something that could end up in someone's home. I needed more intimacy and I realised through 'photography in action' that I could create an image of how I felt, or that I had in my heart and head, more directly. I dint feel romantic about just being a suffering painter.

I also felt that the two painting teachers I was assigned as personal tutors in my first year at Chelsea were only interested in style, not content. I remember telling one of them that I dint want to speak to him because after he saw my first couple of paintings he told me that everybody had problems with their mothers and that I should just get over it. So 3 months later when he came back to talk to me because I was on his tutorial list I told him not to bother. He was not happy and some of my fellow students thought I was out of order, but I remember telling him that I dint come to Chelsea to be patronised by middle class people. I do remember, however, that towards the end of the first year, my second tutor did look at my work and say 'I like this – bravo – make another 10'.

By then I had decided that painting was too restricting for me (although I still see myself as a painter, even though I am painting through sculpture, video, photography and performance). I felt that performing the image that

I wanted to paint but could not paint was more satisfying and immediate, and was what I needed at that time. So I started to make films and video installations to talk about the things I felt or wanted to talk about it. I realised that I could create images like in paintings but using mixed media and films.

When I left Chelsea in summer of 1990 I carried on working on performances for the camera in my flat in Brixton, and I started to go to the now defunct Filmmakers Co-op. But it wasn't until 1994 that I actually performed live in a club, the now legendary FIST run by the infamous Suzie Kruger. She had seen some of my short films and photographs of performances and insisted I performed there, so I took the plunge and did it and felt liberated. After that I never looked back. Slowly I started to build an audience – an arty, cluby, punky and queer following. Performing in clubs like FIST and Torture Garden in the early days was very good for me in terms of losing my inhibitions, and I believe if artists can do clubs like this when they are starting out then they can perform anywhere.

Although I was 'underground' I became quietly famous and in demand as a performance artist, but I dint want to be defined by just one medium or technique and continued working with video, film and installation.

In my performances it was important for me not to lose my dignity or the integrity of the image I was making. The integrity of the image was important, not only as I thought of it beforehand, but actually during the work. Anything can happen and change – and in my view with a live work you can never be in control of its unveiling - as long as the integrity of the image is not compromised. You need to trust yourself to be honest, and trust the audience to be so too.

One of the early themes for my video, installation and performance work, and that stayed with me for most of the 90s, was this intense feeling of missing something. So much of my work was about what it was that I was looking for and what was missing - not just missing a person or a nostalgic moment, but more about looking for some meaningful state or sense of fulfilment. It was not about what I, or others, had not got, but what was missing, which of course is so difficult to quantify by merely using material and petty bourgeois ideals or desires.

But I realised that to search for what is missing somehow 'we' have to share what 'we' have got first which is 'our' self in its most naked, vulnerable state. To be able to *mostrare* [show] and to be able to receive, we must be able to give.

During the most part of the 90s I partied like there was no tomorrow. I had friends that were working in fashion and once a year or so I attended one of their 'catwalk shows' - especially shows by Arthur Peters, Jessica Ogden, and Susanne Deeken. It was one of Deeken's shows for the Ghost fashion house that inspired me to use the aesthetics of a fashion show in performance. The year must have been 1998 and her new collection was presented in the context of a visual art private collection gallery - not just any private collection but the one owned by the renowned 'art collector / dealer' Charles Saatchi, back when it was located in St. John's Wood. Seeing this show in a 'high art' context made me think about fashion, its politics and its contexts and influenced me to use the catwalk as a metaphor and a motor for a performance I made in 1999 and performed many times until 2005.

In 1993 I had met Philip, who became my first stable partner over a period of 4 years. Our relationship was very much an open one. In 1995 Philip and I moved from St George's Residence on the Front Line, to another housing co-operative in Waterloo, but by this time we were just casual fuck buddies living in separate apartments in the same housing block.

Around late 2005 I was at the end of a 4 year relationship with a boy called Kris. One day, Kris told me that he wanted a dog. I dint want a dog as I was travelling a lot and I was worried that nobody could take care of him, and our relationship wasn't going so well. But at the end I agreed, and so on Kris's birthday, the 16th of November 2005, we collected an 8 week old Jack Russell and I called him Beuys. I dint take into account that I would fall desperately in love with Beuys and so he would with me. Soon after, Kris told me that our story was over as he was in love with some girl he had met in Croatia, and he left me. It was January 2006 and I decided to take care of Beuys. Me and Beuys become literally inseparable; it was just the 2 of us. It was not easy at first but we were happy.

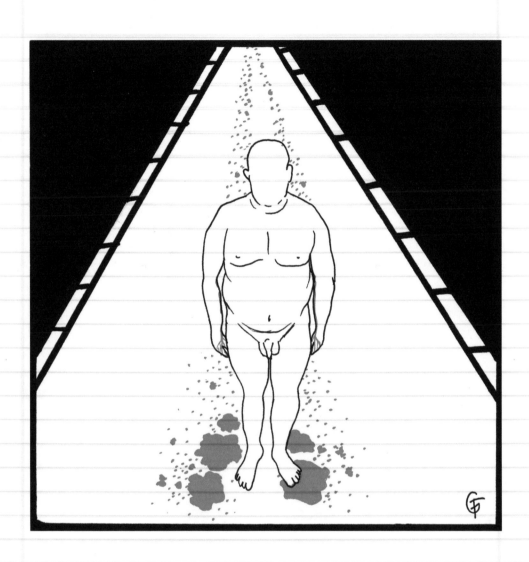

Franko brings life and art together, encouraging you to confront your own truths, working with the seed of a painful memory to exorcise the sadness... It's a kind of transformation, it's alchemical...

Shabnam Shabazi, artist and enabler

At Chelsea his massive paintings were legend, as was his generosity. He shared everything – coffee, pasta, friends. Photographing an ICA performance for publicity for a show in my gallery Last Orders, in Hoxton in the 90s, I met his friend David, who I married. Just as well I hadn't married Franko several years earlier in a marriage planned for his convenience!

Pia Randall, artist

During the summer of 2006 I had selected 10 artists that had just finished their degrees for a mentoring course lasting for a year. Among these students there was Tom Qualmann. Tom looked so different from the others. He seemed so calm and so sure about himself. I couldn't stop looking at him all the time; I liked him and I guess he soon realised it. After three weeks I told Tom I had feelings for him. Even though he replied that he fancied me, he was more worried about our relationship as teacher and student. In the end, we sorted out the student / teacher problem and, at the beginning of 2007, we started to see each other. Around Valentine's Day I decided to get another dog, Rothko, as a companion for Beuys because he was getting more and more jealous of Tom and I thought if he had a friend it may help. In May 2007 Tom moved into my flat and, on the 2nd of October 2007, we became civil partners in a ceremony in Brixton Town Hall.

In May 2008, Tom, the dogs and I went to Italy. First stop was Milan, where I had an exhibition with the Chinese artist Zhang Huan, then to Macerata, at the Accademia di Belle Arti, where I presented my work after the request of a student who persuaded the school to invite me. That day 300 people attended.

Five months later the Accademia di Belle Arti of Macerata contacted me again, this time offering the position of Lecturer in Sculpture to me, as the previous one was retiring. Not all of my prospective future colleagues / lecturers were too happy about me teaching there, but the director insisted and I was accepted through the national application process, which I won because of my CV.

In 2008 I had also received an email from the Italian consulate saying that one of my stepsisters was looking for me and had contacted the Italian consulate to see if they had a record of me in London. She wanted to know if I was ok, and if it was ok to pass my contact details to her.

The stepsister in question was Monica, one of the twins (the one more together than the rest of my family). I decided to try to engage with her at least. So we had a few Skype meetings and it was pleasant. I kept communications open with her and her kids for a while, then in 2013 I decided to visit her with my filmmaker friend Nathaniel.

We decided to document the journey from Milano to the town of Bellusco, where she lived, and then to Omegna to see Raffaella and then down to Macerata to the academy. This was because Nathaniel wanted to make a documentary about my work and life for a course in films he was doing.

We went first to the old place where I briefly lived during my second spell with my mother at the Cascina la ca' Frazione di Lesmo. I have to admit it felt weird, and everything seemed much smaller.

The house where I lived with my mother was still there but looked done up. It was a bright orange colour. The courtyard seemed very small. Across the road the houses where my Neapolitan friend and the boy Enrico had lived were not there anymore. There were instead some smaller houses, like cottages.

I realised how everything was so much nearer to each other in terms of distance than I had experienced before. I walked about 100 metres to where my stepfather's mother had lived, opposite the Molteni meat factory, but it was a building site with unfinished works. The factory had another name and I couldn't figure out what they were producing now. The smell of animals that I remember was gone and the sounds I remember were not there.

I walked to where the Pizza da Franco was and that was now a Chinese restaurant and a pizzeria. 30 metres up the road I visited the car accident repair garages that Mario owned, where I had my first job after the Red Cross Institute. It was closed and I felt Mario was still there but I dint dare or want to make my presence known to anyone.

It dint take long to walk around the small places, with Nathaniel filming me and asking me questions. I felt irritated, yet I went with this purpose, so I could tell my story. I felt emotional but abstracted at the same time; for sure I dint care (or had never cared) for the place.

Then I went to the local police station in Arcore where I tried to report my family for abusing me. Here as well, when I was in front of the place I felt kind of vacant. It was not a cathartic experience as I might have wanted (did I want that?).

Act-Up meetings, the 121 Centre in Brixton, private views
in your flat, early shows at Heaven and in Milch, fierce
performances in the ICA and the best live art experience of
my life when you catwalked the Tate Modern. Great memories,
thanks Franko, love you man.

James B.L. Hollands, curator

Franko B 用犀利的眼光看待世界，用尖锐的作品直戳历史和社会
现实。"爱"是他的源动力，也是他最令我感动之处。----张洹

With a sharp look at the world and straight
works to poke history and social reality.
Franko B expresses "Love" as his source of power,
that is what is touching me most.

Zhang Huan, artist

Franko's blood performances have had a
profound influence on my own work: the
combination of horror and beauty illustrate
the fragility and mystery of life!

Sheree Rose, artist

What is, I think, so special about Franko, and
which one can perhaps relate back to his early
experiences of his childhood in Italy, is that he
is not afraid as we all know to talk about love.

Sarah Wilson, Art Historian

In my kitchen I have Franko's drawing *My Heart
Hurts*. In my toilet I have Franko's shirt which has
a merchandise label saying Clansman and a cut-
out heart filled with red vinyl. One recognises
comrades travelling with one, however similar or
different their manifestations. The recognition
is beyond work, beyond life. It is the connection of
continuous searching, where joy and sorrow dance
defiantly together. It is work of the heart, where
the thought process permeates the whole being,
tender and passionate.

Anne Bean, artist

That night me and Nathaniel stayed in a hotel in Monza, then visited my stepsister Monica the next morning, who was expecting us. The next morning we made our way to Bellusco. This would be the first time in 22 years I would have seen her or any members of my so-called blood family.

I promised her that I would only visit her as long she dint reveal this to any members of the family. I was not ready to have contact with them. She agreed not to tell anyone. Still I was a bit apprehensive. Eventually we found the place, a bit outside the town centre of Bellusco, and rang the bell.

There she was, my 'little' stepsister, the one I had to look after when she was a tiny baby girl in the late 60s and in the mid 70s.

She has 3 kids now; one is living with his father and the other 2 are still at home with her. They are still young: one is 8 years old and the other 12 years old. It is quite an emotional experience and a bit awkward, especially for the kids. I never met them before, and also there is a guy filming this moment that maybe should be really private. At the same time it is something for me to take away, apart from the memory; some kind of evidence that I really did come from somewhere, even though that somewhere is not established by a physical place, but by blood ties.

We stayed for half a day there: talked, hugged, cried, talked, ate together and took photos, filmed, and left.

Next stop was to Raffaella, the woman that looked after me in the first 2 years at the Red Cross, but this was not the first time since then that I had met her.

When I started this biography, I enlisted the help of a UK-based Italian woman called Nina. Nina would come to my flat in the mornings for a few weeks while I would tell / dictate to her my story and she would write it down. Once at home she would Google names and places I told her about and, by chance, she found a 'Raffaella' – an artist that painted the town of Omegna, which happened to be very near the lake of Mergozzo where I was at the Red Cross. As it happened it was the same Raffaella that took care of me 40 years before, and now was an artist. Nina also found her studio telephone number, so I rang.

After leaving a couple of messages, she responded and we reconnected by her coming to London to meet me and coincidently to see me performing at the Laban Centre in London. The piece was a work-in-progress of a new performance called *Because of Love* which was inspired by this very biography. This was 2012, and the performance covered the period from 1965 (the beginning) to 2011, exactly where I left this writing till now.

After Raffaella come to London I went to visit her with Tom and Beuys and Rothko for few day in the summer of 2012. It was very nice; I met her 2 grown up boys, Francesco and Alessandro, and her husband Massimo who I had met 40 years previously, when they were dating each other in Mergozzo.

This time, we arranged to visit her and film her about our past. And there was a surprise that Raffaella kept for me.

The surprise being that we were going to meet Luigi, my old teacher at the Red Cross Institute, and the dentist that fixed my teeth while I was there (he happened to be Raffaella's uncle through her marriage to Massimo).

It was not the first time that I been back in Mergozzo, to the old institute where I spent 4 years of my younger life, but it was the first time that I was there with people that took care of me, in one way or another, while I was there.

The deputy mayor of Mergozzo very kindly opened the institute / building for us so we could go around and revisit the places inside: the classrooms, the dormitories. Except that it was not any longer the Red Cross Institute for poor, messed up kids. The Red Cross left the place and closed the institute down in the mid 80s and now it was a primary school. All the dormitories were transformed into classrooms. The outside was exactly how it was when I left; maybe it looked more depressing, more grey.

My old dormitory where I spent the last 2 years – the white house – was now a canoe club, as the institute was only 100 yards from the lake. Also the little chapel that we had to attend church in every Saturday afternoon was now a recreational social space club for school parties.

So after 38 years exactly, I re-encountered Luigi, my old teacher. He brought with him a picture that I had made while I was there and that I had given to him. He brought it to show me that he still had it. This was sweet; I had totally forgotten it.

It was nice reminiscing about our times there and the different things we could remember or not remember. Also the dentist, now in his late 70s and with advanced Parkinson's Disease, was really nice and he remembered me.

After this stop, me and Nathaniel drove to Macerata in the Marche region of Italy where I was still working at the academy. I had organised with some colleagues a 3 day symposium on performance art with the title *Corpo and Crudelta* / Body and Cruelty. And I had invited to talk and perform: Ron Athey, Fam, Sarah Wilson, Adrien Sina, Ivana Spinelli.

This was a brilliant time at the academy. The students as a whole were very interested in what me and others were trying to do, to actually bring international performance and art to Macerata.

Apart from my stepsister Monica I'm not engaging with other members of my blood family. My stepfather died 3 years ago and I simply dint feel it was necessary for me to be present at his funeral.

My mother is about 78 years old now and I tried to engage with her in an honest way via my stepsister Monica but I realised that it was futile and destabilising for me and everyone involved so I decided not to carry on.

After 7 years teaching in Macerata I left the academy in 2016 to transfer to the Academy of Arts in Turin where I am still teaching. I felt I had done my time in Macerata and had completed a 'cycle' through the education system machine... Many students have started their journey in art with me.

Me and Tom work as artists. We both still make art and have exhibitions. I have a studio at Artsadmin in London. I been there for around 17 years now, and been living in the housing co-op in Waterloo for over 21 years. We are happy and lucky.

Art saved my life and gave me a purpose. Art gave me the confidence I needed to find to use my voice. Art has given me a life. It was not easy, but it did.

TOM'S STORY

During the summer of 2006 I had selected 10 artists that had just finished their degrees for a mentoring course lasting for a year. Among these students was Tom Qualmann.

On the 4th of December we had the first meeting with the new students and those who had just finished, and had a chance to talk about their experiences. Tom looked so different from the others. He seemed so calm and so sure about himself. I couldn't stop looking at him; I liked him and I guess he soon realised it.

After the meeting we all decided to go to a pub and have something to drink and try to socialise. Coincidently, at the end of the pub thing, Tom and I ended up getting the same bus. He then had to get another bus though, in order to get to his sister's house (that was the second coincidence, as I remember Tom once coming with his sister when I had an open studio). After three weeks I told Tom I had feelings for him. Even though he replied that he fancied me, he was more worried about our relationship as teacher and student.

I tried to see him by inviting him around my place for New Year's Eve, but he refused. Later he told me he wished he had come.

Tom and I, in the end, sorted out the student / teacher problem and we started to see each other. At the beginning of 2007, Tom eventually came to my flat, where we started to talk about ourselves, our lives, about art… it was then we decided to keep our professional life separated from our growing personal relationship.

Later in April 2007, during a workshop with all the mentoring students, Tom and I decided to tell everybody about our relationship. Soon afterwards he moved into my flat and in May we told Tom's parents. They were cool and very nice. We also told them we wanted to get married later the same year.

On the 2nd of October 2007, Tom and I had a civil partnership ceremony in Brixton Town Hall. Tom invited all his family, though a few of them couldn't come as at that time they lived in Thailand and Australia. Clare, one of Tom's sisters who was living in London at that time, came with her partner Barney. I invited friends who I considered family and who could be in London for it.

After the ceremony, 30 of us went to Strada, an Italian chain restaurant close to Waterloo.

In 2008 Tom decided to go back to studying. He applied for a masters course at the Slade art school, part of UCL, and was accepted.

On the night of the 9th of May 2010, I said goodnight as usual to Tom and went to bed earlier than him. This was common; I tended to crash by 10pm and he would carry on working in the living room on his work and his final masters show. As the end of the course was close he was spending most of the night awake - he was under pressure.

When I woke up the morning after, Tom wasn't next to me, which was unusual, but I supposed he was still working hard.

It was Sunday; I turned myself over and fell asleep again. After (I guess) no more than an hour, I woke up again as Beuys was trying to vomit next to me on the bed. I quickly left the bed and picked up Beuys to take him into the kitchen so he could be sick there.

As soon as I passed the living room I saw Tom lying on the table, without wearing his shirt, and his work to the side. I thought he was sleeping, though by now Beuys had stopped seeming as if he was going to be sick, so I went to Tom and tried to wake him up. I realised something was wrong. Tom's body was cold, very cold. He looked in an unconscious state and the table was covered with dribble.

I then phoned 2 friends of ours who are doctors, but they dint answer. Eventually one of them, Paddy, phoned me back and made his way to our flat as he lived near us. As soon as Paddy seen Tom, he told me to call an ambulance.

Ron was in London and so I called him to come immediately to see if he could help with the dogs. I jumped in the ambulance with Tom, and when we reached the hospital Tom was taken straight to the emergency room. Doctors were trying to reanimate him but Tom was in a coma and after two hours they finally came to me where I was waiting to explain Tom's status. The doctor asked me to contact Tom's parents as he was in a serious risk of life.

They moved Tom into ICU and allowed me to visit him for few minutes: he was intubated everywhere. I was in shock.

Fortunately Shabnam (a friend of mine who lived near us) come to help me and give me support. I was in total shock.

As this was happening, I had to call Tom's parents. It wasn't a pleasant task. Like me, they were in shock, but in a couple of hours they were already in London. We went to the hospital intensive care unit and after a while we were allowed to see Tom, two at a time.

When it was my turn I got into the room with Tom's father. Suddenly Tom moved and after a few seconds he started vomiting blood.

He had liver, kidney and brain failure; as his liver stopped working, his body was being poisoned and he was bleeding everywhere... and he was alive just because different machines were operating instead of his kidneys and liver. Basically the doctors then told us that Tom wouldn't make it. They gave us 24 hours.

That night Ken, Tom's father, spent the night with me in my flat and Jackie, Tom's mother, with their son in hospital. She would not leave her son's bedside, and so she dint for the next 2 and a half months, also without leaving London, even though her house was one and a half hours away.

I also had to phone Tom's school (the Slade) to let them know what happened to Tom, and tell some of his closest friends, who came the day after to visit him. The doctors weren't optimistic.

After a while they decided to move Tom to another hospital; a special unit of Kings College Hospital in Camberwell, as that hospital had a ward specialising in liver failure. And transplants.

He was connected with so much machinery that it needed 2 ambulances apparently to move him the 3 miles from St Thomas's in Waterloo to Kings in Camberwell.

About 3 days later me and Tom's parents had an important meeting with the main consultant liver intensive care specialist at Kings. She explained how they were trying to keep Tom in a stable condition and how she wasn't sure at this stage if he'd be ok.

She would not or could not exactly predict anything: if Tom would ever be able to wake up again, or if he did, what the damage to his brain would be, and the possibility that we, the closest relatives, could face the decision to disconnect the equipment that was keeping Tom alive.

Tom stayed 3 weeks in an induced coma and once the doctors decided to wake him up, it took three more days for him to regain consciousness. 4 weeks had already passed. Tom's liver, even though in a bad condition, seemed to be working, although the prognosis was that one day he might have need for a liver transplant.

'At a later date' was one of the terms we kept hearing.

He had to put his name on a very long waiting list, unless it was a matter of life or death.

---

7 weeks after the incident and Tom seemed to be getting better and better. He was doing physiotherapy as he had laid in bed for a long period, and everybody was positively impressed by his recovery. Even very impressed.

Soon he would have been able to move from intensive care to the rehabilitation ward, where he would have spent at least 6-8 weeks. But the day before Tom was supposed to move to another ward, he started being sick again.

The doctors decided to do some tests and because the results weren't good they then decided to put him in an induced coma again, so they could manage the new emergency better and give themselves time to understand the reason of this relapse.

Somehow the decision moved to an emergency surgical examination and once done, the surgeons realised that Tom's clinical status had turned worse than expected. Tom's gall bladder had stopped functioning because the liver cord had wrapped around it and stopped the blood supply to it; this had started to poison his body. Moreover, Tom's liver had become very small and stopped functioning on its own again, therefore the only possible chance Tom had to survive was an emergency liver transplant. In fact, the surgeon that opened him up decided not to close the wound while a call was made nationally for a liver that would be compatible with Tom's blood group.

There was a meeting with some of the doctors. They told us that Tom was put on the top of a list for a transplant. They said there was about a 72 hour window that this should have to happen in. If it dint, Tom would die.

At 2 am, I received a call from the duty doctor who informed me that he dint think Tom would make it to the next morning.

Yet, the following morning Tom was still alive...

Hours and hours were passing by while the doctors were trying to get to the right decision as the risk, mainly, was the fact that Tom's body was so weak that perhaps it wouldn't be able to take the transplant even if they got a new liver for him

In the end an internal committee of specialists decided to approve the transplant on the basis that it was a life or death situation and the fact that Tom was a young man and that would work in his favour.

It took 80 hours to find a liver suitable to Tom. But it happened.

As it was getting very desperate, Tom's parents phoned me saying that the hospital had tracked down a liver suitable for Tom from a 68 year old man who died the previous night, somewhere in Britain. The surgery lasted 10 hours and Tom was moved again to intensive care.

Four weeks after that, Tom moved to the rehabilitation ward and less than 3 weeks later he come back home. It was the 30th of July, his weight was

88 pounds and he was taking something like 60 different pills to keep him alive. A week later all Tom's family, me, and our friends celebrated Tom's 27th birthday in a park near the hospital. We had a great day and great memories. It was a new beginning for all of us.

Tom nowadays is fine. He gained the right weight... He takes 2 pills per day which help his body not reject the new liver, and he has to go to the liver clinic at the hospital every 6 months.

Eventually he also went back to the Slade to finish his masters, and perhaps by coincidence he finished it the same day exactly a year after he received the new liver. He finished with a distinction.

After Tom's liver transplant scare and stress, I actually suffered from what they call 'existential depression'. I was on medication for about 4 years. At first it seemed a miracle had happened with the medications, but it dint last; the side effects and need to continue changing medications turned my life into the worst nightmare. I was even more depressed on them.

Eventually I managed to come off the medication with the help of a understanding doctor, and after 2 years off them I have started to feel better - the side effects of the medication are finally wearing off. Now, although it can be difficult sometimes, I have come to accept that at nearly 57 years old my existential doubt and depression are realities that are to be expected.

Franko is looking at me.
I don't know what he wants, but he knows, and he is certain.
There is an intensity in his gaze, a sense of urgency.
His mood informs his perception.
He is deeply affected by what he witnesses.
He is still looking at me.

Tom Qualmann, artist and partner

BEUYS' STORY

Beuys came into my life on the 16 of November 2005. He was about 8 weeks old when I picked him up from a family in south London as a birthday present for Kris, my then boyfriend / partner.

Kris had suddenly told me that he wanted a dog. I dint as I was travelling a lot and I was worried that nobody could take care of him, and our relationship wasn't going so well, but at the end I agreed to get a dog with him. Maybe I believed that a dog could revitalise our relationship, and so on Kris's birthday we collected a Jack Russell puppy and I called him Beuys.

I remember he fitted in the palm of my hand and in my jacket pocket, and was so small that I dint realise that the family he come from had docked his tail with elastic - it was only a few weeks later that I realised this had happened because someone in the street accused me of doing such a thing and abused me about it.

Straight away I realised that Beuys was going to become more my dog and my responsibility. The first night with us, Beuys cried all night until, in order to make him sleep, I put him just right on my chest and we both fell asleep. This become a regular way for Beuys to go to sleep. I became his mother.

I dint take into account that I would fall desperately in love with Beuys and so would he with me. Soon after, Kris told me that our story was over as he was in love with some girl he had met in Croatia, and he left me. It was January 2006 and I decided to take care of Beuys.

It was just the 2 of us alone for almost a year and we became literally inseparable. It was not easy at first but we were happy. Whenever I was invited to deliver a workshop or a lecture or a performance or an exhibition Beuys would come with me, and when this was not possible or practical, it started to become a problem.

151

While I was learning to drive it was not possible to take him with me, so I would leave him at home alone and Beuys would let me know that he was not happy by pissing and ripping my bed mattress to bits.

I decided to take him to a dog trainer, and once even a specialist dog behaviourist came round our flat saying that Beuys felt that he was the boss of the house and I should do something to change this status quo. The specialist dog trainer gave me some good advice and things to do that helped address the situation, but he also told me some things that I dint agree with, like 'don't let him sleep in the same bed as you', which I ignored.

He also added that I needed to be trained more than the dog as I was too attached to Beuys, even though the trainer admitted that he had never seen a human and an animal so bonded to each other. I needed some help but I dint want a rigid dog / owner relationship.

Beuys took over my life really and in many ways he also saved it.

I was running a mentoring scheme with 10 artists for a year and Beuys would always come with me to meetings with them and with other people I was meeting for work.

Everybody loved Beuys, but at first he was a bit jealous of people when I was not giving him the full attention.

I remember bringing a home a German boy called Ralph and Beuys pissing on him while we where lying in bed after sex. He also did this to Tom a few months later when we started seeing each other - he would bark every time me and Tom touched each other or kissed. Eventually this stopped and Tom became part of Beuys' and my family.

I remember when I started going out with Tom telling him to never try saying 'its me or the dog' because I would always have choose Beuys.

Very early on in my relationship with Tom I decided that would it would be a good idea to get another dog so Beuys would be less jealous and have company.

So on Valentine's Day in 2007 I got a Jack Russell Parson and called him Rothko.

Rothko and Beuys were my favourite artists when I started making art so I honoured them by naming my 2 dogs after them.

Rothko, Tom, Beuys and I lived together for almost 10 years. We were a family.

Both Beuys and Rothko saved our life together many times in terms of focussing on what was important - routine, family, distraction, depression, love and intimacy. Without a doubt they helped keep this family together.

And Beuys did actually save Tom's life by waking me up when Tom fell into a coma while alone in our living room in May 2010.

After 11 years in my life, Beuys got sick with cancer in his mouth and deteriorated very quickly. 6 weeks after the diagnosis of his illness, we had to put him to sleep on Boxing Day of 2016. He could no longer eat or drink because of the cancer.

Even though Beuys has left us he will be always be in our hearts. We want to celebrate him in the most happy way possible. Yes I was heartbroken to see him deteriorate so quickly and to have to put him to sleep (because it would have being to cruel to keep him alive), but his memory and his spirit will always keep him alive to me.

Live long in our hearts beautiful being x x x

Beuys

5/10/2005 - 26/12/2016

PEOPLE

I would like to thank all my friends and people and things that made this book possible, and that supported me in all my life period and still do, and those who consented to allow me to use their story in my story.

While at Chelsea School of Art I met many people, students, lecturers, administrators... some of them were amazingly supportive, but also prepared to challenge me and what I was doing and the way I sometimes was behaving. I will always be grateful to these people for their friendship and support, for caring, sharing and for their love: Urik Bock, Ali Zaidi, my fellow student and friend James Hutchison (a great person and an artist that I had a crush on), David Hepher (the then-head of painting, generous teacher and lovely man), Helen Chadwick, Brian Chadwick (who recently passed away), Nigel Rolfe, my dear friend and teacher Anna Thew, the head of alternative learning media Stuart Marshall, Tim Mara, Shelagh Cluett, Gerard Wilson, and Steve Burry, the librarian. I also have to thank my friends outside art school like Oliver and Keith for inspiring me and pushing me to perform live.

In 1995, at a friend's funeral / death wakening, I met Ron Athey for the first time, and we became friends and brothers. Ron is an American artist for whom I have great respect and love. In 2009 he moved from Los Angeles to London and stayed for about 5 years. This was great for those of us in London that love him, but he missed his sunny California and moved back there in 2015.

157

In 1995 I met also Lois Keidan. Lois was at that time the director of Live Arts at the Institute of Contemporary Arts in London. Lois had heard about my performance work in clubs and alternative arts spaces and asked me if I wanted to perform at the ICA. Originally my answer was no, because I felt that the ICA was too commercial and an art ghetto. Lois assured me that it was not and thanks to her and this context, and the timing, my work became known and talked about outside the small underground scene that I was navigating in before. I'm so glad that I listened to her and accepted the offer to perform at the ICA in what turned out to be an amazing programme and opportunity for me to show my work.

In 1997 I met Gilles Jobin and Maria Ribot (La Ribot), 2 choreographers and artists very different from each other in temperament and work, but also married to each other. They had a little boy called Pablo and we become very good friends.

I performed for camera for a new piece of work by Gilles called A+B, which was a piece of work that I loved and in my view one of the best works Gilles made that I have seen. Also me and Gilles briefly became collaborators and did some performances together: 2 or 3 pieces in dance festivals in Europe. I think we did very good work together overall but both agreed that we were difficult to work with. We remain good friends.

Also, one thing for sure was that collaborating with Gilles helped me with gaining confidence and self-respect in regards to how to deal with financial transactions in art. He introduced me to Artsadmin in 1999, an organisation that for many years has produced and promoted experimental theatre and dance, and also produced some of my performances in London. Artsadmin gave me and younger artists so much support over the years, and in my case it also gave me a bursary and an affordable studio where I could work and produce objects and performances freely, and after 18 years I'm still there (mainly thanks to one of its directors Gill Lloyd, who has been like a big sister to me many times).

In 1997 I met Francesca Alfano Miglietti ('FAM'), her husband Cesare Fullone and their daughter Giuditta, who was about 4 years old. FAM and Lois Keidan became very important people in my life: their friendship, love, professionalism and astute eyes helped my development as a person and in my artistic practice. After 20 years of friendship, with its ups and downs, I still have this immense feeling of love and respect for them.

Lois lives in London and FAM in Milan and in terms of art history I consider both of them the Lea Vergine of the XXI century (thanks to FAM I actually had the honour to meet influential art critic and writer Lea Vergine and she is adorable!).

Another close friend that I consider part of my family is Riccardo Barba from the city of Verona in Italy (but I met him in London in 1999). We became collaborators. He had a company – at that time, a pioneering one – that was working exclusively with resin in interior design and also producing artist works in resin. This led me to set up a studio near his workshop for nearly 4 years as he was producing a lot of my work for the art market.

I finally want to thank Shabnam, Mayu and Sean, Ron, Lois, Mickey and Nathaniel, other friends and Tom's family who were so brilliant with me and Tom and the dogs while Tom was in hospital. They were next to me all the time and are still my friends.

Franko B's practice spans drawing, installation, performance, sculpture and curating. Over the years he has built up a diverse and substantial body of work and has gained international acclaim for his contribution to contemporary culture. He lives and works in London and is Professor of Sculpture at l'Accademia Albertina di Belle Arti di Torino, Italy. He has presented work internationally at Tate Modern; ICA (London); South London Gallery; Arnolfini (Bristol); Palais des Beaux Artes (Brussels); Beaconsfield (London); Bluecoat (Liverpool); Tate Liverpool; RuArts Foundation (Moscow); Victoria and Albert Museum (London); Freud Museum (London); PAC (Milan); Contemporary Art Centre (Copenhagen) and many more. His works are in the collections of the Tate, Victoria and Albert Museum, South London Gallery, the permanent collection of the City of Milan and a/political, London.

Giuditta Fullone graduated in Modern Literature at Università Statale di Milano and in Screenplay at Milan's Civica Scuola di Cinema Luchino Visconti. Her production ranges from illustrations for publications and magazines, to graphics for advertising, logo-design and mural paintings. She has also participated in the organisation of artistic, fashion and entertainment events. She is currently attending DAMS's Cinema and Media Masters degree at Università di Torino.

David Caines is a graphic designer and visual artist based in London. Other books he has designed include: *Kira O'Reilly: Untitled (Bodies)* (2017), *People Show: Nobody Knows But Everybody Remembers* (2016) and *Out of Now: The Lifeworks of Tehching Hsieh* (2009/2015). David also makes paintings and in 2015 was shortlisted for the East London Painting Prize. www.davidcaines.co.uk

The Live Art Development Agency (LADA) is a Centre for Live Art: a research and knowledge centre, a production centre for programmes and publications, and an online centre for representation and dissemination. LADA is funded as a National Portfolio Organisation by Arts Council England.

CREDITS

Because of Love
Franko B's Story

First published in 2018 by
Live Art Development Agency (LADA)
The Garrett Centre, 117A Mansford Street, London E2 6LX
www.thisisLiveArt.co.uk

Edited by Lois Keidan, with Megan Vaughan
Illustrations by Giuditta Fullone
Design by David Caines Unlimited

Front cover image by Raffaella
Back cover image by Hugo Glendinning

Printed and bound by Pearl Print Management

ISBN: 978-0-9935611-5-3

LADA and Franko B would like to thank Adrian Heathfield,
Tim Etchells and Mark Stephens CBE for their advice and
support in making this book possible.

**Live Art
Development
Agency**